Mama Told Me

Mama Told Me

JOYCE HOUSE McDONALD

as told to her by Katherine M. House

MOUNTAIN ARBOR PRESS

MOUNTAIN ARBOR
PRESS
Alpharetta, GA

This book is a work of nonfiction. Unless otherwise noted, the author makes no explicit guarantees as to the accuracy of the information contained in this book.

ISBN: 978-1-63183-360-1

Printed in the United States of America   1 1 2 9 1 8

♾This paper meets the requirements of ANSI/NISO Z39.48-1992 (Permanence of Paper)

Scripture quotations marked "NASB" are taken from the New American Standard Bible®, Copyright © 1960, 1962, 1963, 1968, 1971, 1972, 1973, 1975, 1977, 1995 by The Lockman Foundation. Used by permission.

All photos are believed to be part of the Power, House, and McDonald family archives, unless otherwise indicated.

All quotes are Mama's unless otherwise indicated.

For my mama, and her mama, Mary Lillian Power Morris, whom I loved but never knew, but grew to know through the writing of this book; and for the generations to follow. May those who follow, follow the Lord.

Tell the generation to come the praises of the Lord and His strength and His wondrous works that He has done.
That the generation to come might know, even the children yet to be born, that they may arise and tell them to their children that they should put their confidence in God.

—*Psalm 78:4b, 6–7a (NASB)*

Contents

Acknowledgments

My thanks to Mama for bravely sharing her story.

And to all the aunts, uncles, and cousins who listened to me and answered my questions.

To my family, who has heard me say for years that I was going to write a book, and for their encouragement.

To Sarah, my granddaughter, for editing—such a big help.

To my brother, Lee, for proofreading and his most valuable editing suggestions.

To Anne Alexander for her time and expertise in editing.

To Sandra Bean for her remarkable work on the family genealogy.

To Aubrey Morris, whose research was a rich source of information.

To Sallie Anderson Miller, daughter of Elizabeth Power Anderson, sister of Samuel Wesley Power, who wrote down what she remembers that her mother told her.

To Annette Lindsey, Bob Roland, Mike McCrum, and others at Fellowship Bible Church who shared their memories of the early days at FBC.

To the Lord for telling me over and over "to write." His patience is amazing!

Introduction
Mama's Story
— Putting the Pieces Together

Oh God, Thou hast taught me from
my youth; and I still declare Thy
wondrous deeds.
—Psalm 71:17 (NASB)

"I love you," he said. No one had ever told her that before. In all her sixteen years, she had never heard those words. Of course, her family loved her. She knew they did. Her family was not one to show affection that way. But he swept her off her feet, and her love and devotion for this handsome young man would be real and lasting. But let me go back and tell you the story about Katherine Margene Morris before she met Bennie Lee House.

My mama has told me the story of her life. Not all at once, mind you, but bit by bit through the years. I think it is important to say how Mama revealed her childhood to me and my brother. She was very careful to tell funny stories that were appropriate for children when we were young. Wisely, she waited until I was forty to tell me the painful things. Now, I think I have a pretty good idea of the world in which she spent her childhood.

It was not easy for my mama growing up in the '30s, having been born in 1928 and into a family that had seen more hardship than one family should have to bear. How did my grandfather do it? Mama doesn't really like to think back to those days, but every now and then something will slip out. When she gets started, even though a lot of it is painful, she tells me how it was and how she felt. She'll say, "I don't like to think about way back then," but then she'll start and go on and on.

She is the youngest girl in a family of nine siblings. Mama would correct me on that point. "There were eleven of us," she'd say. "L. B., who was named after my daddy, died when he was two, and David Hugh died as a baby." Now, being the youngest girl, she knew she would probably have to watch the older ones go to their grave. I think she hid that thought in the back of her mind. As it has happened, she has buried seven of her siblings, not counting the two who died young. Six of her in-laws, some of their children, her son-in-law, and her own precious husband are with the Lord as well. I guess it is time for me to try to put it together now and see if I can get it all straight. So here goes. I hope I get the facts and emotions down on paper. It is hard to believe her story, but it is true.

Chapter 1
The House on the River

For Thou didst form my inward parts; Thou didst weave me in my mother's womb. I will give thanks to Thee for I am fearfully and wonderfully made.
—Psalm 139:13–14a (NASB)

April 14, 1924

"I don't feel well, Luther," Eugenia said on that morning in April. "It doesn't look like I'll be able to make you a birthday cake." It was my grandfather's thirty-second birthday, and their new baby girl was only eight days old.

My Great-Grandma Power lived in the old Power family place on one side of the Chattahoochee River in Fulton County. Luther Burney Morris and Eugenia Elizabeth Power Morris, with their six children, lived not far down the road from Eugenia's family on the west side of the river in Cobb County.

This land had been in the Power family for over one hundred years.

A quick look back and we can see how my family came to live on that land. According to the book *Sandy Springs Past Tense*, by Lois Coogle, the Creek Indians yielded the land to the United States government on January 8, 1821. It was divided into five counties: Dooly, Fayette, Henry, Houston, and Monroe. Each county was divided into districts. Men who wanted to draw in the land lottery and who met certain qualifications had to take out a grant to the lot he drew and pay nineteen dollars for each grant (*Sandy Springs Past Tense*, 11–12).

My great-great-great-grandfather, James Power, was granted the land in that lottery. My great-great-grandfather Samuel Wesley Power's sister, my Great-Great-Aunt Elizabeth, had a daughter, Sallie Anderson Miller. She recorded what her mother told her about her grandfather, James Power. Some of the information that was passed on to my family is included here:

> He was born in Laurens County, South Carolina, on April 15, 1790. He fought in the war of 1812. He came to the Chattahoochee River in 1826 and the Cherokee Indians were on the north side of the river. The Indians could ford the river on horseback. James could fix guns, shoe horses, fix wagons, and do most all kinds of things. The Indians were very friendly with him and visited him often and he visited them. When he did something for them, they paid him in corn. He knew the names the Indians called certain animals. A trilla was a horse, a dog was a skeener, a cow was a walker. And honey from a beehive was known as water lacy. James received a land grant on the Chattahoochee River, and he moved there in the 1820s. He was the justice of the peace and was called Judge Power. He and two other men rode horseback to Milledgeville, the capital of Georgia at that time, to secure the charter for Marietta. He married Samantha Hopkins (his second wife), who was from Greenville, South Carolina. James was fifteen years older than Samantha. She was born November 22, 1805, and died July 1, 1891, at age eighty-five.

James built a ferry to cross the Chattahoochee River. He and his sons operated the ferry for years. There is a road today named Power's Ferry. According to Sallie A. Miller, "A ferry was a boatlike vessel, long enough for two two-horse wagons with mules hitched to them. It was hand-pulled by a heavy wire stretched across the river and securely fastened to big trees on the banks of the river. They called this vessel a flat."

James had been married before, but we don't know much about his first wife except that they had a son, my great-great-grandfather, Samuel Wesley Power. Note that the name was Power, and the possessive form is used of the ferry. Another note to mention here is that Samuel Wesley Power fought in the Civil War, and his uniform and gun were on display at the Atlanta History Center for years, but now are stored in the archives. Samuel was born in Cobb County, July 13, 1830, and died there December 18, 1916, at the age of eighty-five. He married Mary Ann Hopkins, who was born March 23, 1828, and died November 24, 1908, at age eighty. Samuel Wesley and Mary Ann had six children, and my great-grandfather, Samuel Adam Power, was number five.

Samuel Adam Power made the third generation to run the ferry. He married Margaret Samantha Spruill. James and Wilson Spruill, Samantha's relatives, along with several other families, started the Methodist church in Sandy Springs. In 1851 Wilson Spruill gave five acres for the church, which had been meeting in an arbor (*Sandy Springs Past Tense*, 13). It was the site of the present-day United Methodist Church, 251 Mount Vernon Highway. Samuel Wesley Power was the first man to join the Methodist church in Sandy Springs by a profession of faith. The church held revival meetings, and everyone from miles around would come to these meetings, called camp meetings. The young people loved to go because they were able to meet others their age.

It was on that April morning in 1924 that my grandfather decided he had better take his wife to the hospital. The pain in her side just kept getting worse. As he was carrying her to their wagon, she told him the pain had stopped.

She said, "Take me back to the house, Luther. I'm fine now."

"We need to go on to the hospital," my grandfather insisted.

They met the ambulance at the end of the dirt road to the house.

Mama wasn't told how they got word to the ambulance driver, but Mama's sister, Bernice, was with them in the wagon and told Mama this was how it happened.

The children were left at home with Grandma Power. She married Samuel Adam Power, but he, at age forty, had tuberculosis and died. So, in 1908, at the age of thirty-three, she was a widow with eight children.

Now in 1924, her oldest daughter, Eugenia, was sick and in pain. Grandma Power still had five children of her own at home: William, Grady, Lillian, Wesley, and Alice. Grandma Power would send Lillian over to Eugenia's house to help with the small children. Lillian would stay with them while her sister went to milk the cow or do other chores. Eugenia had birthed six babies before this last one and nothing like this had ever happened. Ethel was eight; Bernice, seven; Fred, six; Grace, five; Sallie, almost three; L. B., two; and now the new baby, just eight days old, named after her mother, Eugenia Elizabeth, and called "Genie."

Aunt Pauline, who was married to Luther's brother, Ben, took the newborn, "Genie," to care for her when she was six days old.

Eugenia Power Morris left that morning, never to see her newborn or their other children again. The pain had stopped when the appendix burst, but gangrene developed. At the hospital in Atlanta, Eugenia died of appendicitis. The last thing she told her husband was "Luther, keep the children together."

They built her casket on the front porch of the house.

The funeral was at the Methodist church in Sandy Springs. All the children sat on one pew with their daddy on one end and Eugenia's sister, Lillian, on the other. What a sad day for the two families! There were seven siblings of Eugenia's to mourn her passing: Ruby, Fannie Lou, Lillian, William, Wesley, Alice, and Grady.

Eugenia and Luther had a very sickly two-year-old, L. B. Jr. He had been this way all his short life. He was born prematurely and was so small and weak that people marveled at his size. Eugenia would carry him around on a pillow. She had taken him to the camp meetings at the Sandy Springs Arbor (where the Methodists held church), and everyone was concerned. Only his mother seemed to know how to take care of him. Now that she was gone, his condition steadily got worse. There was nothing the doctors could do, and he died two weeks after his mother.

Ethel, the oldest, was in Alpharetta staying with Grandma, Charity Rhoda Jett Morris, and Grandpa, William Burney Morris, when her mother died. She could help

Grandma even though she was only eight. Grandma Morris was in a wheelchair. She fell between horses that were hitched to her wagon and broke her hip some years before. It did not heal like it should and left her crippled. Ethel told Mama that Eugenia sent a letter and a dress she had made for Ethel to Grandma Morris, finished except for the buttons. Grandma was able to finish it for her. Ethel was living with them so she could attend the school near the Morrises' house on Mid-Broadwell Road. Grandma Morris had been a schoolteacher, as was her sister, Aunt Georgia Ann Cates. Aunt Georgia Ann also ran a rooming house for teachers.

After the death of their daughter-in-law, Grandma and Grandpa Morris moved from Alpharetta to that house on the Cobb County side of the river, even bringing their livestock to help their son. Grandpa Morris was seventy-four and Grandma Morris was seventy-one when this move took place. Luther was the youngest of seven boys and five girls. Aunt Georgia Ann came by to see how they were doing, and Grandma Morris told her everything was going fine except for Bernice, who would not mind and was always jumping on the bed. Aunt Georgia Ann said she would take Bernice with her and make her mind.

Mama was told that Aunt Lucy, Luther's sister, had also given birth and was nursing her son, Bobby. Genie was taken to stay with her for a short time, so Aunt Lucy could nurse her too.

Lillian was used to helping out at her sister's house, and what a blessing she was.

Luther was working night and day just to keep food on the table. He worked along with his father and brothers at the sawmill. His father was in the sawmilling business before him. They would buy land and cut the timber, then move to another piece of land. Luther was a very good sawyer. According to Webster's Dictionary and my mama, a sawyer sawed the wood into planks and boards.

1926

As so often happens, Lillian and her brother-in-law, Luther, found their affection had grown in the two years since Eugenia's passing.

Lillian was the fourth child born to Samuel Adam Power and Samantha Spruill Power. Lillian was an excellent student. Her artistic ability was outstanding. Mama still has some of her drawings and schoolwork done at Crossroads School, as well as her diploma. Lillian graduated from Crossroads School on May 5, 1915, when she was sixteen. It was located where Dupree Street and Mt. Vernon Road intersect near Power's Ferry. They simply called it "Crossroads."

Around 1922, Lillian came down with typhoid fever. She lost all her hair and the family was in quarantine. Eugenia walked to her mother's house to help take care of her younger sister. She took her own children with her but would not let them go inside, so they played outside and said they remembered seeing the nurse leave after her visit with Lillian. Nursing care was provided, but you had to pay dearly for it in those days. Thankfully, Aunt Sallie Spruill Whitfield, Grandma Power's sister, helped financially. While Lillian was sick, she read everything she could find. Mama said she was told that "she read one book right after the other."

Mama told me how her mama, Lillian, and Lillian's sister,

Alice, were so close. Alice told her daughter, Margaret Bruce Jordan, that she and Lillian were sisters, yes, but also best friends. They won blue ribbons for the beautiful canned goods they made together and took to the fair. They knew just how to place the items in the jars to make them look "so pretty." Margaret and Mama have been close too, all their lives. They talk on the phone at least once a week, even now.

When the day came that Luther announced to his children that he intended to marry Lillian, the children did not like it. Grief does funny things to people. The children did not know to be thankful for Lillian's presence; they just felt the absence of their mother and brother. They would play tricks on their aunt/stepmother, like putting too much black pepper on her food after she fixed her plate and other such pranks that made her life miserable, according to Mama's sisters. Mama told me that they looked back with regret that they acted this way.

Luther built a new house for her up the road from Grandma Power's place. Mama refers to this house as being "out in the country." It was just on the other side of Shellnut's Dairy near Powers Ferry in Sandy Springs. He bought these three acres from Aunt Georgia Ann.

Instantly, now, married to Luther, who was thirty-four years old, Mary Lillian Power Morris, at the age of twenty-seven, had an entire family of her own to raise, and of course more babies would follow. Lillian gave birth to David Hugh, but he died in infancy. They say he smothered in bed with his parents.

1927

Just about a year after Luther and Lillian buried their first child, on June 19, 1927, Luther's father, Grandpa Morris, died at age seventy-eight. Mama never knew him, as she, Katherine, was born on April 28, 1928. Dr. Griffin delivered her at home. Jerry Myers came along on October 14, 1929. Then Grandma Morris passed away on November 13, 1931, age seventy-eight, just a couple of months before Charles Edward was born on February 12, 1932.

The family had now grown to nine children. To say that Lillian had her hands full is an understatement. She had to go to the branch to get water for any purpose. (A branch, according to Webster's Dictionary, is a tributary stream running out of or into a larger stream of water.) She had to wash clothes by hand. That meant making a fire and boiling the clothes while using a "battling stick" or a "punching stick" to stir the clothes and remove them from the washpot. She used a scrub board to get the clothes clean, all done down at the creek. She cooked on a wood stove and had to milk the cow twice a day, all while taking care of all the children.

"Once," as Mama recalls, "I was standing next to the fireplace and my clothes caught fire. My mother came running and jerked my dress up and off so fast. I was burned, and I still have the scars under my right arm and down my side. They took me to Alma Pittman, who was known for being able to 'talk the fire out.' My mother saved my life!" Mama recalls that "Genie got burned too. She was standing in a chair trying to reach the shelf behind the wood stove. The chair was sitting on a piece of firewood and was not sturdy. It gave way and she was burned all under her chin and down her neck."

When Charles was six months old, Lillian started behaving strangely. They always said typhoid fever had settled on her brain and she never quite got over that. Mama was four and a half years old, and Jerry almost three. Lillian's behavior got worse and it was determined that she needed professional help after she bit her mother. Mama said her sisters told her they realized "her mind was slipping." Maybe it was post-partum depression. Who knows? Lillian suffered a complete mental breakdown and was institutionalized. The police came to take her away. "She wouldn't keep her shoes on," Mama remembers. "She was sent to the State Mental Hospital in Milledgeville."

There were no highways back then. It was a long trip to Milledgeville, so the family rarely visited their mother. Mama remembers taking her a birthday cake one time. I remember visiting her once when I was little. She loved kittens and Coca-Cola. She had beautiful skin and white hair, the color of Mama's and mine. She didn't know any of us, and that made me so sad. It was hard on Mama to see her mother like that. I always dreamed of bringing her to live with us, which was, of course, impossible. I know that now, but as a child I didn't understand.

She remained there until her death, July 26, 1972, approximately forty years. Mama said, "It was just easier to let people think my mama was dead, rather than tell them what really happened. I felt like I was living a lie until I was old enough to realize that God had a plan for my life. Many times, I think about it and start to feel sorry for myself until I think of what my father went through."

Lillian's brothers and sisters were as follows as Mama tells it: "Ruby, who married a Chapman; Fannie Lou, who married a Chapelier; William, who married Nettie Squall; Wesley, who married Lelia Waldrop; Alice, who married a Bruce; and Grady, who married Emma Hamrick."

Chapter 2
Scattered

His eye is on the sparrow, I know He
watches me.
—Civilla Durfee Martin (1905)

If you will remember, the years we are talking about are the years following 1929—the Great Depression. Times were hard, real hard, and a man who has all these mouths to feed has got to get money somehow. Luther Morris, my granddaddy, owned his own sawmill and did odd jobs of all kinds to provide for his family. At one point, he and his brother-in-law, Grady Power, started selling moonshine. It landed Luther and Grady in jail.

All the children went to Uncle Ben's and Aunt Pauline's when this happened. They were such a sweet couple. Uncle Ben dug out a cellar and put beds down there for the children. I remember Aunt Pauline, and anyone who knew her remembers how she used to say, "I declaaaaaare" in a high-pitched voice.

Later, the children were scattered to different places. I know Luther must have thought about Eugenia's last words so many times. She knew that he would need help. Bernice was already living with Aunt Georgia Ann. Aunt Georgia Ann's second husband was Charles Cates. Bernice loved "Granny Cates," as she called her. That the feeling was mutual was apparent to everyone. Bernice always said her daddy never came to get her. Truth is, he knew she was better off there.

Grace went to live with Aunt Bertha and Uncle Glen Morris, Luther's brother. He raised the best yellow-meated watermelons. Mama told one story about Uncle Glen. He was plowing and went down to the spring to get a drink. He took out his false teeth and put them in the water to soak and left them there. He went back to plowing. When they called him for lunch, he went to get his teeth and couldn't find them anywhere. He looked and looked. Finally, he found them up under the bank of the spring where a crawfish had carried them.

Fred and Sallie stayed with Aunt Pauline and Uncle Ben, as did Genie. "Genie had a box under the bed with clothes in it and a doll," Mama remembers. Aunt Pauline and Uncle Ben had three daughters, Frances, Dot, and Mary. Ben Jr., their only son, served his country and was killed in World War II. "Fred ended up at Aunt Grace's, Luther's sister. Ethel went to live with the Pattersons, where she was trained to be a nurse. She went on to be their nanny."

Mama and Jerry went to a foster home, Mrs. Clebo's. Mama was five years old. She remembers that Mrs. Clebo took her and Jerry to see their siblings at Uncle Ben's house one time.

The Clebos only had one car, so Mrs. Clebo would pick her husband up from work in "big downtown Atlanta." Mama and Jerry would go with her. Oh, the lights and neon signs! There was a "Big Pig" at the Pig and Whistle grocery store and a big horn, which was the whistle, all lit up and flashing! Mama said it was wonderful.

Then Mama and Jerry went to a children's home in Atlanta, called Hillside Cottages. Mama tells about taking only a few things to the home, and one thing was a doll that she loved. Every now and then some kind people would take them home for a visit. Mama remembers driving through Atlanta one time and seeing all the pretty Christmas lights. She also remembers having a feast at either Thanksgiving or Christmas. "Our eyes were as big as saucers looking at the table all full of good food."

Jerry was the youngest one at the home. They would dress him up with a top hat and he would walk in front of a person in an elephant costume and doff his hat. Everyone loved it. "He is so cute," they would say. While living at the home, the boys stayed in one cottage and the girls in another. Occasionally and happily, Jerry and Mama would run into each other and they would hide in the bushes to talk. They wondered where everyone else was and if they would ever see them again. They didn't know where Charles was. Later they learned that Luther's sister, Aunt Grace, took him to her house. Mama loved to memorize poetry. Mama remembers swinging on the water pipes in the basement. "They did have some fun," she said.

Chapter 3
Together Again, Almost

Great is Thy Faithfulness.
—Lamentations 3:23 (NASB)

1932

Two years later their daddy came to get them at Hillside Cottages. The children went to school while there and the teachers encouraged them to save their money. They each had a bank account at the school. Mama had twenty-eight cents in her account, and when Ethel and her daddy came to get them, they went to the bank to get her money. They told her the account was so small they had closed it. She remembers the amount still today because that was a lot of money to her at that time. Also, they would not let Mama take her doll. They said any toys that came there must stay there. It broke her heart.

Mama's daddy gathered up his children from all over and they were together again. They went to live with Aunt Grace Swofford, one of Granddaddy's five sisters. The five girls from oldest to youngest are Lucy, Grace, Allie, Mary, and Georgie. Aunt Grace lived on Faith Street, close to Grant Park. When her husband died, she sold the property that she had inherited from her father, which was located across from the old Morris place on Mid-Broadwell in Alpharetta. There is a church there now. Aunt Grace decided to move to Atlanta, where she could get work because she had to raise her children: Doris, Lorene, and Elizabeth. She went to work in a pants factory. It was to this house in Atlanta that Luther came with his children. The older children went to Faith School and they all started going to Faith Methodist Church. For a while, Granddaddy worked as a janitor at the church. One Christmas Eve they went to church, and when they got home, Santa Claus had already come. What a surprise! It was a great Christmas. Mama can't remember what Santa Claus brought, but she remembers the joy they all felt.

Aunt Grace's daughter, Elizabeth, married Tom Duffy. Their daughter, Evelyn, was Mama's age and a good friend as well as cousin. They lived down an alley and around the corner. An alley was "an unpaved road," Mama explained. It was so wonderful to have a friend close enough to visit regularly.

Another memory of those early years was of going to school with Genie. In those days, they would let brothers or sisters go to school with an older sibling. "Just one time, though," Mama said.

Mama remembers they would get to buy a popsicle occasionally, the kind with two popsicles together with two sticks. If it had the word "free" written on the sticks, then you got a whole new one for free. One time Mama won a free popsicle and she gave it to her sister Genie. She remembered how she felt, bursting with pride being able to do that. As she told me this, I could see that look of pride once again cover her face.

Luther loved to chew plug tobacco. The brand he liked was Red Mule. It had a little red mule made from metal on the wrapper. Mama took one and wore it as a pin. Granddaddy just laughed.

Granddaddy worked for the Works Progress Administration. The WPA was part of the New Deal in which the government employed millions of people to work on projects, such as building roads and public buildings. He was on the crew that built the Cyclorama in Atlanta. That is where the huge mural depicting the Battle of Atlanta, when Sherman came through during the Civil War, was displayed.

Mama also remembered to tell me that one Father's Day, Luther had the most children at church, and he was awarded a Bible by the preacher, Pastor Callaway.

1933

The next move was back to the house that was next to the dairy on Power's Ferry Road—"out in the country." It was while they were living here that Mama recalls her daddy making charcoal and selling it.

This is quite a process. Mama had told me about this process, and her brother—my Uncle Charlie—explained more about it. Oak was preferred, but they mostly used pine. They would dig a hole with a post-hole digger about eighteen inches deep. They put kindling in the bottom and placed a sapling (a young tree that was around seven feet tall) in the hole. Then they stacked dry logs around the sapling and kept adding logs—making it a round mound about twenty feet in diameter with an opening where you could light it. Pine straw covered the mound, and on top of the pine straw they placed dirt, always leaving an opening at the top like a teepee so it could breathe. Ashes from a previous fire went on top of the dirt. They took a long pole and wrapped paper around it to light it. You had to watch it all through the night to make sure it didn't break out. Then you added more dirt to keep it contained. It burned for a week, depending on the size. It was a three-week commitment. It smoldered until it burned out. Once it burned out, it collapsed from seven feet high to about four feet. This was called a "coal kiln" (the children pronounced it as a "coal kill"). The next step was to get a lot of water to sprinkle on the mound to put out the fire. They used a pitch fork called a "coal fork" to spread it out on the ground. They made piles all around the perimeter of the fire and sprinkled water on each pile (as needed) to make sure it was out. The children helped with sprinkling the piles. The coals were then put in bushel or half-bushel baskets, to take to Atlanta to sell—where the Atlanta Stadium, Turner Field, area is today. They went door to door selling it. They would stand up in the back of the truck and yell, "Charcoal!" People would buy it for fifty cents a bushel.

Fred, the oldest boy, used to go over and help Mr. Shellnut milk cows. He would also go hunting and bring home rabbit or squirrel to cook. Their mailing address was Dunwoody, Georgia, Rt. 1. Ethel, Fred, Grace, Sallie, Genie, Katherine, Jerry, and Charles were all back together again. Bernice was the only one not there because she was still at Aunt Georgia Ann's. Mama remembers that Ethel made seventh-grade graduation dresses for Grace and Sallie. She went down to Mrs. Shellnut's to sew. They were beautiful, light-blue dresses. Mama told me, "Ethel could make me a dress out of one yard of fabric. Ethel bought a doll for me and made clothes for it. The doll had a trunk and a blanket. The doll would fit in the trunk with all its clothes. It had a carriage too, and I would push that doll all up and down Power's Ferry Road."

Ethel would go to Paul and Kelly Jordan's to stay from

time to time. She always came back to help with the children "out in the country" (Power's Ferry). Mama remembers her sister Ethel whistling "Red Sails in the Sunset" while she heated the water and got Mama's bath ready. As Mama told me this, I could tell it was such a sweet memory that it made her happy to remember it. Since Mama was the baby girl, she looked up to her older sisters. They were like mothers to her, and she is so grateful she had them. At the same time there was a void and the constant reality of missing her own mother.

Every spring the older girls would clean out the fireplace. They knew where they could find some white mud (as opposed to the red clay of Georgia) and use it to paint the face of the fireplace. This is what they called "white-washing." Next, they cut the covers off old magazines that a neighbor had given them, and with glue they made themselves out of flour and water, glued them to a large piece of "pasteboard" (cardboard). Then they placed it over the opening of the fireplace as a fire screen would. "It was so pretty!" Mama said.

Mama, Jerry, and Charles loved to go down to the swampy areas of the branch, or creek. They would cover their legs up to their knees with mud. They walked around and let it dry, pretending they were wearing boots until the older kids would make them wash it off.

There was a large rock above the spring that was close to their house. They had a "buff hen" at that time. It was a yellow chicken that made a nest on that large rock. Charles got great delight in finding eggs in that nest. Mama said, "When a hen laid an egg, she would cackle as if she were so proud. She gave herself away every time."

Granddaddy went frog gigging. He fried the legs and made biscuits and gravy. Tastes like chicken, she says.

Mama told me they would walk to see their Grandma Power, and even when they were a long way from her house they could hear the swing squeaking. "Grandma's swinging on the front porch," they would say.

Mama remembers Grandma Power would always set a pretty table with her Blue Willow dishes. She used these dishes every day. Mama also remembers that Grandma Power was a very strict disciplinarian. No singing at the table, and watch your elbows! She had a farm table with a silverware drawer where she also kept leftover biscuits. Mama loved to visit and ask if she could have a biscuit. Grandma always said yes.

On either side of the road on their way to Grandma's house was Mr. Shellnut's pasture. There was an apple tree in that pasture and sometimes they would get some apples. The girls would use their skirts as baskets. They always had to watch out for Mr. Shellnut's bull. They never wore red if apple picking was in the plan. They were never sure which pasture the bull was in.

One day, Genie and Mama were in the pasture looking for their cow. They were walking the cow home to milk her when the bull came into view. It then started following them and bellowing.

Genie said, "We better climb this tree."

Mama said, "I can't climb that tree!"

Genie said, "You'd better!"

About that time the bull came over the hill. When he got to the top and Mama could see him, she told me with a smile on her face, "I learned to climb real fast." Mr. Shellnut heard the bull and came to see what was going on. He took a stick and shook it at the bull, who finally turned his attention elsewhere.

While living at Power's Ferry, "Fred worked for a company putting up neon signs for businesses in Atlanta. He had to climb way up high. He got very sick with pneumonia and they took him to Grady Hospital. Dr. Johns found out that he was in the hospital and went by to check on him. Dr. Johns was a dentist who had a practice in Buckhead. He was Granddaddy Morris's friend. They went hunting and fishing together. He was good to the children. He brought them gifts, and Grace and Sallie would invite him to stay for dinner. When he left, he would leave a ten-dollar bill under his plate."

When Dr. Johns was told the doctors had done all they could for Fred, he told them, "Oh no, you can't say that. You do something!"

"Well, Fred came home and had to stay in bed and stay warm. Neighbors came and chopped wood, so they could keep the fire going all through the night. He eventually got over it. He did not go back to that job, and not too long after, he joined the army."

Bruce Taylor and his family lived across the river, and he and Fred joined the army together. Fred had dated Bruce's sister, Evora Taylor, and Sallie dated Bruce.

One time the Taylors had a party. They made candy and invited the Morris children to come. They had popcorn and syrup candy. They pulled and pulled the candy until it turned from red to white. It was great fun and a great memory. Grace and Sallie wanted some new furniture like the Taylors had. Granddaddy said they would have to go to work to make some money. It was not too much longer until they decided to leave home to find jobs.

Mr. and Mrs. Harvey Puckett bought William Power's nine acres that he had inherited from his father. The Pucketts had owned property near Georgia Tech, which they rented after they made the move to the country. Mr. Puckett was a retired Atlanta streetcar conductor. Mrs. Puckett held Bible studies in a little building on Northside Drive not far from their house. These Bible studies were much like Vacation Bible Schools that are now held in the summertime. Mama remembers all the neighborhood children came.

One time the Pucketts bought a lot of watermelons. There was a very cold spring by the side of the road to their house, which by the way was lined with beautiful plants and flowers of all kinds. They put the watermelons in the pool of water that collected under a big rock. They invited their friends from Atlanta to come out to the country for a watermelon party on the river. Mama's family was also invited, Mama told me.

It seemed like Granddaddy was always building another house. One time he was building a house on Eugenia's property—years after she passed away. Ethel would fix lunch for him and take it to him. Sometimes she would carry Charles on her back. One day she had a story to tell when she got there. On the way over Backbone Ridge, a snake started following her. With Charles on her back, Ethel ran all the way. Granddaddy said it must have been a coachwhip snake protecting its young. She made it there, though, out of breath, and Charles was still on her back!

Mama remembers when they paved Power's Ferry Road. "They brought prisoners to work on it. They watched them but were not afraid. It was interesting to see them build the road."

She and Genie learned to roller-skate on Power's Ferry Road. That year they got skates for Christmas. One day, Genie skated all by herself, past Grandma's house and across the bridge into Cobb County. There was ice on the sides of the road. She wanted to visit the Taylors. This was a long way, and they were not sure where she had gone. Mama remembers how worried they were and that they marveled that Genie did that!

Granddaddy put a metal pipe in the branch, or creek, as it sloped downhill and it made it easier to get water. They had a bench for the washtub and a clothesline that their daddy put there. The pipe in the branch was a brilliant idea, as well as the bridge he built across the branch.

Mama remembers a time when Genie was standing in a washtub near the branch and she shook a muscadine vine. A snake fell from the vine into the tub right next to her feet. Mama said Genie could really move fast!

They moved almost every year, so just about the time they would make a friend or get used to a school, they would move. Once, Granddaddy came home and said, "Let's load up the wagon." They left with no warning or anything. They didn't even tell the teacher or their classmates they were leaving. They didn't know it themselves until it happened. "This was how it was in the sawmilling business," Mama told me.

1934

When Aunt Georgia Ann, "Granny Cates," died (March 4, 1934), Uncle Ben found Bernice a place with the Holbrooks.

Bernice, age seventeen, met Al Stovall at a square dance. They started going to Sardis Church every Sunday with Aunt Pauline and Uncle Ben. The church was near Chastain Park. Aunt Pauline and Uncle Ben lived on Morris Road between Pole Town and Buckhead. Bernice and Al decided to get married, so they caught the bus and went to the justice of the peace in Marietta. They said their vows and were married on March 26, 1935. They stayed in a motel in Marietta that night. Al had a job in Texas, so they started married life there. Not too long after that, they moved back to Atlanta, where they bought their first home. In 1985 they celebrated their fiftieth anniversary at their daughter, Renee's, home.

Bernice encouraged Sallie and Grace to come live with them.

On the Fourth of July, Sallie and Grace cleaned all day like it was spring cleaning and got supper ready. They fixed peas, squash, other vegetables, whatever they had, and cornbread. They had it all planned. They had walked up to Myrtle Wade's house earlier that week and scheduled a taxi, keeping it a secret. The other children were wondering what all the fuss was about.

Their daddy was down in the bottoms "laying by" the corn. To "lay by" meant to plow it for the last time before harvest. They liked to have all the crops "laid by" by the Fourth. Grace and Sallie had made their daddy a lunch and put it in a lard can with a jug of milk. Genie and Mama were instructed to take it to him.

The taxi came. Grace and Sallie grabbed their things and said they were going to Atlanta to get jobs. So those two young girls had to tell their daddy that the other two had left home. Granddaddy just sat on a rock, under a tree, and didn't say a word. "He was studying this thing over. That night at supper, he was real quiet. He seemed to be thinking hard about it."

Grace got a job and roomed with relatives of the Stow family after leaving Bernice's. That's how she met Walter Stow, whom she later married in October 1939.

1936

Ethel, almost twenty-one, married Ruse Moss on August 5, 1936. They lived in Mobile, Alabama, for a while. Ruse had worked on ships during the war and was able to secure a good job by moving there. Their fourth child, Nita, was born there. Sidney, Erma, and Jo were born in Georgia, before they went to Mobile. After moving back to Georgia, Jimmy, Jayne, and Paul were born.

Mama's next home was at the end of what is now Wooten Road in Roswell, a house with a big barn. Genie was the oldest now, followed by Mama, Jerry, and Charles. Genie did the cooking, cleaning, and all that it takes to keep a family going. Mama said occasionally they would put kerosene in lids and then put those lids under each leg of the bed. That way the bedbugs would not be able to crawl up and get in the bed. She remembers, too, taking the mattresses out in the yard to look for bugs.

Another memory while living in this house was going swimming in a pond at the bottom of a pretty waterfall. Mama started to climb a rock and there was an old car fender that had washed down there. She slipped and cut her foot. It was a very deep cut. Grace and Walter came by and said she needed to soak it in Lysol in a pan of warm water two times a day. She can show you the scar.

They still had "Old Babe," their milk cow. One of the jobs Genie and Mama often had was to watch the cow graze. While doing that, they would do their schoolwork. If it were winter, they would sit up under an overhang of two rocks to stay out of the wind. Sometimes they would build a fire on the rock. Mama said, "I wish I had listened more to Genie. She'd say, 'Study your spelling words,' but I would rather run through the broom sage." Sometimes Genie would say, "Now that your foot is better, you go get Old Babe." But Mama remembers, "It still hurt to walk on it."

Old Babe went all over grazing, and Genie and Mama had to find her at milking time. One time the cow got lost. They couldn't find her anywhere. They went to their next-door neighbor; they looked everywhere. They didn't find her, so they had to wait until the next day to look some more. However, during the search, Mama met her dear, lifelong friend that day, Nettierene Hyde.

Reflecting on what they cooked back then, Mama said if they didn't have anything else, they had eggs. Cornbread and milk or buttermilk was a frequent meal as well. Fred used to trap quails, rabbits, squirrels, and whatever he caught, they ate. He was a good trapper and hunter. One time they even ate possum.

Sometimes, Granddaddy would go off with the Thomasons: Herman, James, and Forrest. Their mother was Lucille, "a wonderful person," who would take Mama, Genie, Jerry, and Charles to Mount Pisgah Methodist Church with them. Sometimes they would stay with the girls when the men and older boys would go hunting or fishing. They were a well-thought-of family. Mr. Thomason was the justice of the peace. Forrest would walk Genie home from church sometimes, but it was Herman Genie really liked. Mama remembers this with a smile.

I asked Mama, "What was it like in the evenings at home?" She told me they would sit around the fire and read or do homework. They didn't have electricity, so they used kerosene lamps. When they were little, in the summer, they would play outside until dark and catch frogs and lightning bugs.

1939

By this time, Fred was in the army. He joined the army just before the war broke out and was stationed at Fort Polk in Leesville, Louisiana. The GIs would go to Port Arthur, Texas, when on leave. That's how he met Betty Duprie, whom he married in 1943. They were expecting their first child before he shipped out to war. Fred fought in the Battle of the Bulge, and he saw General George Patton and his ivory-handled revolvers. His son, Perry, said, he "never remembers his father complaining about the war, his loss of hearing from all the artillery fire, or all of the hardships that he suffered during the fighting." One time an eighteen-year-old in his outfit was hit, and Fred caught him when he fell. The boy died in his arms. When Fred came home they settled in Port Arthur, Texas.

The next move Granddaddy, Mama, Genie, Jerry, and Charles made was from the house with the big barn at the end of Wooten Road to the log cabin at Crossroads in Sandy Springs. This log cabin was "a very nice, well-built cabin," which they rented from Mr. Cates. The cabin had one big room with a very large fireplace. The beds were at one end and the kitchen at the other. The cabin was on Mount

Vernon Highway and was located on a lot behind where a Lutheran church is today. The church sits on what was then their pasture. Once Genie and Mama were on their way to catch the school bus, and Genie said, "You've got the measles! Let's go back home." They turned around and went back, and they put a bed in the kitchen for Mama. Genie complained that she had to stay home from school to take care of her. Mama was about eleven, and Genie fifteen. It was in that same kitchen that Mama told me she learned to make biscuits.

"The government put in a huge culvert under Dupree Road, which we called 'the dirt road.' We used to walk up 'the dirt road' to catch the school bus. The branch, or creek, went through this big pipe. Genie, Mama, Jerry, and Charles loved to slide down that pipe under Dupree Road. Many times, though, they would get there only to find one or two snakes in the slide. They just threw rocks at the snakes and scared them away so they could slide!"

One time, Granddaddy shot in the air and scared them. They had reasons to be frightened. They were not sure what to expect. Many times, he had been drinking. Jerry always said he thought he was shooting at him. So, on another occasion, Genie, Mama, Jerry, and Charles heard their daddy coming up the road to their house. They thought he had been drinking. They went out in the woods and hid in a stump hole. As they were running by the clothesline, they grabbed a quilt that they were airing and laid it down in the stump hole and hid there. They waited a long time before they crept back to the house. They were relieved to see him on the back porch, washing his feet. As it turned out, Cousin Leanna's husband had died, and he was getting ready to go to the funeral. Leanna Dean Moss was Granddaddy's first cousin, daughter of Aunt Georgia Ann. He was not drinking at all.

Her daddy was "a good man, with a pleasant and kind personality when he wasn't drinking," Mama assured me. "His personality changed a bit though when he was drinking."

Chapter 4
Just Four

Remember those who led you, who
spoke the word of God to you . . .
—Hebrews 13:7 (NASB)

1940

It was while they lived in the log cabin that Genie decided to move to Atlanta to go to work. Genie said she felt bad when she thought back to it, because that meant leaving my mama there to take on the care of the family, and she was so young. Genie decided, though, to go live with Frances and her husband, Jamie Norris. Frances was Aunt Pauline and Uncle Ben's daughter. They lived in town, and Genie could work at a meat market at the Atlanta Farmer's Market.

Mama had to learn so many things all by herself. As each of her siblings left home, either to take a job in Atlanta, join the military, or get married, Mama took on more and more responsibility. Mama, at age twelve, was left at home to cook, clean, sew, milk the cow, churn the butter, and wash clothes for her daddy and two younger brothers. Now the family of nine children was down to four.

Getting water from the branch, or creek, was a constant chore. She had to milk the cow, make breakfast, get ready for school, walk to school and back, and fix whatever they had to eat. Then for dinner they would have "maybe some potatoes and maybe some fatback." They just plain didn't have much. Mama said, "It sure was hard to get the gravy out of the groove on a lard can lid." But at least sometimes they had gravy.

Moving all the time made it difficult to have anything nice. They didn't have many dishes, and one time someone gave them some "real pretty ones." Granddaddy came home, and he had been drinking. He threw all of them against the wall and said, "We don't take charity." He was a proud man—even when drinking.

Sallie lived with Doris and Nell Swofford and took care of their daughter, Jean. Nell had a brother, Neal. Sallie worked at a store called Davison and Paxton's, which later became simply Davison's and finally the Macy's we have today. Sallie fell in love with Neal, who worked there too, and it was while they were sitting on the bench just outside of Davison's that Neal proposed. They went to the justice of the peace in Decatur to get their license. They soon married on June 12, 1941.

December 1941

Mama's daddy was not a talkative man, and early on this particular Sunday morning, he was no different. He told the children to turn on the radio. Mama remembers it vividly. Her daddy had heard that something had happened, and it was important. So, they sat listening to the news. The Japanese had bombed Pearl Harbor! She knew when her daddy was thinking real hard about something, and he was thinking hard about this. They all knew what it meant. The United States was in the war! That's what all the talk and speeches meant, World War II! Mama remembers feeling sad, so sad, as she looked up in the sky and wondered if she would ever see an airplane go over again. If one did go over, would it be an American plane, or a plane from another country? They did not have blackout drills like in the big cities since they just had kerosene lamps. They did not have electricity yet. Their radio ran on batteries. Granddaddy didn't get electricity until after Mama was married. So many lives were changed forever that day. The men and women who died at Pearl Harbor gave their all, and their friends and family back home began the journey of grieving. Others were wounded, and they, too, had their lives changed that day. All our lives were affected by this inconceivable action taken by Japan in a war so very far away that had now come home. Many young men decided to enlist. Some were already serving in the military. Some of those brave soldiers were our relatives, and we will be forever grateful. Mama's cousins, Ben Morris Jr. and Gene Long, died on the battlefield. Mama's brother, Fred, was in Germany. Mama's brothers-in-law were in the service. The war would continue and eventually play a big part in Mama's life. Then there was the rationing. Mama said you were given coupons for sugar, gasoline, and shoes, as she remembers it. If they didn't need something, they would share their coupons with those who could use it.

1942

Then Mama moved to another house that was across the road from Mama's sister, Grace, on Holcomb Bridge Road in Roswell. Granddaddy was hired to make syrup for the Long family who lived there. They rented a couple of rooms upstairs with their own entrance. The woman who owned the place, Mrs. Long, wouldn't let them use her clothesline. Mama remembers having to wash clothes by hand and lay them across the bushes to dry. Mama had just turned fourteen, and they had to move again.

Granddaddy built a house on the property his father had left him. It was off Old Alabama Road on one side and off Seven Branches Road on the other side. He had sixty acres but sold twenty acres to Ralph and Lottie Howard. Mama refers to it as the house "down in the woods." Genie would come on weekends to help him work on the house. Mama remembers that "Genie helped put on the roof." Mama told me that she used to gather flowers from the woods around her house and put them inside "to brighten up the place." It was while living here that Aunt Lucy Pannell would take Mama to church. Aunt Lucy lived across the street from the Howards. She went to a church in Roswell, and the members would come out and hold revival meetings in an old schoolhouse that was almost on their property. They had to bring hymn books and everything they needed for a church service—except for the piano, which had been left there in that old schoolhouse. They would invite all the families around the area to come. Aunt Lucy had explained the plan of salvation, and one night Mama went forward and accepted Jesus as her Savior. How thankful we are for Aunt Lucy. God has a plan for everyone, and He uses people to accomplish His work.

While living at the house "down in the woods," Mama raised eight or ten Rhode Island Red chickens. Granddaddy brought home feed for the chickens. Mama did this for 4-H Club. The 4-H Club pledge explains the symbol: "I pledge my head to clearer thinking, my heart to greater loyalty, my hands to larger service, and my health to better living for my club, my community, my country, and my world." She also grew tomatoes as a 4-H project, and her brother, Jerry, raised corn for his. Audrey Hawkins, another student, was assigned the task of going around and checking each student's progress and reporting her findings at each meeting. Mama used an old washtub for her tomatoes. She put red dirt, then topsoil, then seeds. When they got big enough, she transplanted them to the garden.

Granddaddy was a good farmer. He would dig a hole in the side of a bank of dirt and put sweet potatoes in it to grow new plants. Then he would take the "slips," the vines that had grown, and replant them. I even remember going to his house when I was a child and seeing him plow up sweet potatoes behind a mule. He let us go in the field after he finished plowing and pick up potatoes. This brings to mind what Mama said about their neighbor, and my daddy's aunt, Mrs. Gillie Hamrick. She really loved the Lord. If you knew her, you knew she was a Christian. She pieced quilts and sold them. She would ask if she could go over the fields after they had been harvested and see what might be left. Mama said Mrs. Hamrick worked so hard for everything she got.

One day two teenage boys came to see Jerry. Jerry was not home, and Mama was there by herself. It was springtime and all the doors were open. After they found out Jerry wasn't home, they went outside. As soon as they did, Mama locked the doors and watched them. "They were acting funny, and then they tried to get the door open." Now, knowing Jerry wasn't there, they should have either gone home or waited quietly outside. Mama was frightened, so she got her daddy's .22 rifle. She stuck it through a knothole in the door and shot into the woods. They took off running. By the time Mama got to the window to look, they had already made it down the hill. After it was over, Mama got scared again just thinking about what if she had hit them or someone else.

I want to go back and cover where Mama went to school. She attended first grade at Mrs. Clebo's. When she went to Hillside Children's Home, they kept her in first grade. The school she attended after leaving Hillside was the Hammond School in Sandy Springs. She was a student there second through fourth grades. When they moved to Roswell, she attended Newtown School, fifth through seventh grades, and then on to Milton High School.

Mama always talks of the first-grade teacher at the Hammond School, Miss Annie Houze Cook. She had a reputation as an excellent teacher.

This summer, Uncle Charlie called to say that he had seen James Bagwell at his vegetable stand. That reminded Mama of something that happened at Hammond School. James was in Mama's class, and he came in to school one morning and told the teacher his family was moving to "the country." His daddy was a sheriff and was being transferred to Alpharetta. Hammond School was in Sandy Springs. The teacher just looked at him and said, "Where do you think you are now? We ARE in the country!"

When Mama was in third grade at Hammond School, she and another girl were to perform a song during an assembly. She and this other girl got so tickled they could not sing, and the principal had to make them leave the stage. I think when Mama remembers, it still makes her smile, but with a trace of regret.

The Newtown School had three rooms and an auditorium with a stage. It was built in 1929 and is now on the National Registry of Historic Places. Each room had a big bottle of water that Mr. Scott, the janitor, would fill every morning from the spring. He was Vaudice Scott's father. She was a friend of Mama's, and they saw each other just a few weeks ago at the Deree's Style and Barber in Alpharetta. They had not seen each other in years. Mama has been going to Deree for at least thirty years.

At Newtown School, Mrs. Crowley taught music, Mrs. Jones taught geography, and Mrs. Pax Smith, and another Mrs. Smith, were the teachers. These were the members of her class: Dewey Hawkins, Gwen Barber, Oma Purcell, Maurice Campbell, Jerry Morris, and Calvin Long.

Mama recalls how wonderful it was when Mrs. Pax Smith would tell the children to bring their cups and spoons tomorrow because she was going to heat up the food that the government had sent. She would place a big can of pinto beans in a pan of water on the pot-bellied wood stove and let it heat all morning. Then they would all have a wonderful lunch. Sometimes they had canned grapefruit. There was no cafeteria, of course, and they brought whatever they could find from home. It might be nothing more than a leftover biscuit or cornbread. Most of the time they didn't have anything to eat at school.

Sometimes the bus driver, Hubert Reeves, would stop at Hawkins Store, and if any of the children had a little money, they could buy a candy bar. Audrey Hawkins's family owned the store. She and Mama were in 4-H together, and Mama recalls jumping rope with her. Mr. Reeves would say, not one time, but every single time, as the children left the bus to go to the store, "Turn your hat around so I'll think you're coming back."

One day, Matt Brown said something he should not have said, and the teacher literally washed his mouth out with soap. She gave him a glass of water and said go out on the porch and rinse it out. They didn't have a sink or anything. This only happened one time—at least that Mama can remember.

The teacher asked what the capital of Turkey was, and Dewey said, "Gobble, gobble." He thought he was so funny. Even the teacher laughed.

"Granddaddy traded the forty acres we lived on to Bill Loner for the property off Old Alabama Road." The road that is Wooten Road today was our driveway back then. There was a big house that Mama said she loved. She even enjoyed "sweeping the yard." They would take two or three dogwood saplings or a bundle of sticks and tie a string around them to make a brush broom. They didn't have grass; they just swept the ground.

Mama remembers her friend, Dorothy Morgan, who had very curly, brown hair. She lived at the end of their driveway, on Old Alabama Road. Her dad was a mechanic, and sometimes on Saturday, he would give them a ride to go to the movies in Roswell. Dorothy, or Dot as they called her, was one of seven girls, no boys in her family. They would "pile into her daddy's old truck, happy to get a ride and have some fun."

I've been amazed at the details Mama remembers about her childhood—so many years later—like this one. The Morgans had a cow, and they let it graze in Granddaddy's pasture in the daytime. They would get it at milking time, keep it until morning, and then return it to pasture.

There were many times in her childhood when they would get nothing for Christmas. Sometimes they got only an orange. If it had been a good year, they might get a pair of shoes and socks. I asked Mama about having a Christmas tree. She said sometimes they did, but most of the time they didn't. One year, though, Granddaddy took them to pick out a tree. They didn't have decorations, but they made some out of sweetgum-tree balls. They covered them with shiny chewing-gum wrappers they found on the side of the road. They managed to make decorations, and "That tree was beautiful!" Mama also remembers that she, Jerry, and Charles were given some roping to decorate the tree. Each one thought they could fix it better! One would put it on and the other one would take it off and say, "Let me fix it right." They did that over and over. Mama just laughs when she tells that story. "They had a lot of fun with that tree."

Mrs. Gillie Hamrick's daughter-in-law, Totsie, wife of her son, Raymond, was out for a walk one day, and she stopped by to see Mama. She asked Mama if she had ever baked a cake and Mama said, "No." Totsie told her how to bake a cake, and Mama made her first cake that day!

Granddaddy had a cotton field, and Mama and Jerry were in the field, picking cotton. Mrs. Gillie Hamrick and Warren, her husband, were paid to help pick cotton, and she said to Mama, "If you'll go kill a chicken and put it on to stew, I'll come in and make some dumplings for all of us." Mama and Jerry got one of their chickens and killed it. "Then we got some water from the spring, put it in a big pot, got it to boiling, and put in the chicken. Next, we pulled all the feathers off, then gutted it and cleaned it well. Finally, we got more water, cut it up, and put it on to stew."

Mrs. Hamrick told Mama she would eat anything my mama ever cooked because she was so clean. Mama remembers that "those chicken and dumplings were so good!" Mama loves to work in the kitchen, and everyone knows what a great cook she is!

Sometimes they had a creek or a branch for their source of water, but at other times they had a spring. There is a difference between a branch and a spring, as Mama explained. A spring is just a small area where the water would spring up from underground and make a small pool of cold, clear water.

One of Mama's most precious memories is overhearing Grandma Power telling Grace and Walter that "Katherine, Lillian's daughter, turned out to be such a beautiful young lady."

Genie got a job at the Peachtree Hills Pharmacy at the soda fountain. When the kids would come in and sit down for a treat, they'd say, "Ice cream, Gene." She and one of her friends would often date soldiers. This one time it was supposed to be a blind date, but the young man said, "I'd better take a look at her first." So he looked out the window, saw Genie, and said, "I think she'll do." On September 28, 1944, Genie married Virgil Tilley, a handsome soldier from Iowa. They lived on Tenth Street in Atlanta, and for a few months at 2199 Stephen Long Drive, before moving to Iowa.

When Grandpa Power passed away, he left each child some land. They wrote the parcels on pieces of paper and put them in a hat. Then the children drew for their share. Granddaddy got two draws, one for Eugenia and one for Lillian. Granddaddy paid the taxes for years on this property, but eventually, he sold his first wife's land and divided the money among their children. Genie was not yet twenty-one, so her money was put in a trust. Bernice bought her first car, Ethel bought a milk cow, Sallie bought a piano.

Mama doesn't remember what Fred and Grace did with their money.

Genie said when she got married, she felt like she had a gold mine because of her trust fund, and she was now of age. She and Virgil left Atlanta on December 15, 1945, in a 1936 five-passenger Ford convertible. They drove it to Iowa, with baby Joe, to a farm near Virgil's family. Almost three years after their first son was born, a second son, Daniel, joined the family.

Chapter 5
A New World

For this cause a man shall leave his
father and his mother, and shall
cleave to his wife . . .
—Genesis 2:24 (NASB)

1944

"When I was sixteen, I met my husband," Mama said one day.

I asked her, "How did Daddy propose?" She looked back to that special day with a smile.

Mama and Daddy's paths had crossed a few times. Once Daddy was with his first cousin, John Albert, at Nettierene's house. She also saw him another time at his Aunt Gillie's house when he came up there from Atlanta to go hunting. The Lord does work in mysterious ways. Aunt Gillie's brother, Wes House, was Daddy's father. Wes House had three sisters. Daddy's mother, Isabelle Manning House, had two sisters and four brothers. One of Wes's sisters married Isabelle's brother. Their children were double cousins! So Daddy and his first cousin, Annie Mae Manning Little, were related on their mother and their father's sides. Also, John Albert's sister, Margaret, married Daddy's mother's brother, so John Henry Manning was Daddy's uncle and first cousin by marriage. Mama told me that these facts always made a good story.

Mama said one time they were on a double date. She was with John Albert, and her friend, "the dollar girl," was with

Daddy. They called her "the dollar girl" because one night they were taking her home and right there in front of her driveway was a dollar bill blowing around—and they got it. They called her "the dollar girl" from then on. Anyway, that night they were on the double date. Mama was with John Albert in the back seat and Bennie was driving. He looked in the mirror, and she happened to look in the mirror at the same time. Their eyes met, and they knew. It was magic!

In the fall, my mother said, "Mrs. Gillie Hamrick had a going-away party for her nephews, Bennie House, who was drafted into the army, and John Albert Jones, who was drafted into the navy. Because Roswell was a country town and it was hard for young people to meet, she invited the neighborhood teenagers to come.

"Aunt Gillie rolled up the rug in the parlor so they could play Spin the Bottle, a very common party game at this time. When it was Bennie's turn to spin the bottle, it landed on Katherine. Aunt Gillie and her daughter, Christine, were there to make sure it did. According to the rules of the game, the couple had to take a walk, and he was due a kiss. As they walked along the top of the hill, her hair blowing in the wind, he asked her to wait for him. She said she would."

The following spring, the spring of 1945, when he came home on furlough from basic training at Camp Blanding in Florida, he gave her a diamond ring. They wrote for the entire two years he was in the army. They wrote almost every day, talked of marriage, and made their plans.

During those two years Mama worked in Buckhead at Earle's 5 and 10 Cent Store, 264 Peachtree Street. Nettierene worked there, and she told Mama about the job. She was sixteen and made twenty dollars a week. She still has the

W-2 form from that job. She rode to and from work with Bill and Annie Mae Loner, who owned an upholstery shop in Buckhead—behind Jacob's Drug Store. She paid them to ride with them, of course. They would walk to Jacob's Drug Store and get lunch. "A bowl of soup cost twenty cents and all the crackers you could eat." Mama remembers buying a dress at the dress shop up the street for seven dollars. She worked Monday, Tuesday, and a half day on Wednesday. Sometimes on Wednesday, the girls who worked together would go to the movies. It was a whole new world indeed.

It was her first job, and she worked in notions and Nettierene worked in hardware. This store also had a candy counter and a personal hygiene section. The manager, a man, wanted Mama to talk to another employee who worked in the hygiene department. He didn't feel comfortable to address the subject. The woman really needed to use deodorant. Mama asked her if she used deodorant. The young woman said, "No." Mama told her that it would be so easy for her to get some since she worked in that department, and then she suggested, "You can get some, go to the bathroom, and use it. Just tell them to take the cost of it out of your paycheck." She did what Mama suggested. That was a clever way for Mama to approach that coworker with that touchy subject.

One day, Mama woke up in a great deal of pain. Her tooth was hurting severely. Her daddy said to go ask Annie Mae Loner, their neighbor, if she was going to Marietta that day. She said yes, she had some errands to run, and that she would take Mama to the dentist. The dentist pulled her tooth, but it was already abscessed. Back at home and still in pain, Mama had to milk the cow and do her other chores, but then her jaw began to swell up more and more. Nettierene came to see if she wanted to go out in the snow, but of course she didn't feel like it. Mama told Ethel, who lived close, about her tooth. Ethel told Grace, and after talking to the doctor by phone, Grace's husband, Walter, brought some ice to put on her jaw. Mama couldn't even open her mouth. Grace and Walter lived on Holcomb Bridge Road, not too far from Mama. They called for an ambulance, which was the hearse from the funeral home. It doubled as an ambulance. Bill Loner, Annie Mae's husband, took her to meet it. She was taken all the way to Grady Hospital in Atlanta, an hour's drive at least. She was there eight days.

They had to make two incisions under her jaw and chin to insert tubes to drain the infection. Her whole head was "bandaged up like a mummy," she said. Mama couldn't wash her hair. That was very hard on a young girl. She still has the scars from the operation, and even though the doctors wanted to do plastic surgery on her to eliminate the scar under her chin, she told them she had to get back home to take care of her daddy and younger brothers. Her daddy and Charles came to see her one time while she was in the hospital. Genie and her husband, Virgil, borrowed a car and came to see her while she was at Grady. Virgil was in the army, but since he was in the hospital at Fort McPherson for a heart condition, they were able to visit her. Genie gave her stationery and stamps so she could write to Bennie.

Neal, Mama's brother-in-law, Sallie's husband, was in the navy, but he happened to be home for Christmas. Sallie and Neal lived with Neal's sister, Nell. Her husband, Doris Swofford, was in the navy too, and they were both home on furlough. Neal picked Mama up at the hospital and took her back to their house. She would have weekly doctor visits for a while, so she stayed with them since Sallie lived at Brookhaven, which was much closer to the hospital than Roswell. Mama had to go several times to get her chin redressed. The trolley stop was beyond the railroad tracks from Sallie's house, and as she walked over the tracks, she dreaded riding on the trolley with her head all bandaged. Every time they would say, "Come back in a week." She was there through Christmas.

Sallie did not have a present for Mama for Christmas. Mama didn't have a present at all, and after everyone had opened their gifts, Nell left the room and came back in and said, "I did have something for you." She gave Mama two pairs of underwear. Mama didn't know for sure, but felt she must have bought them for her own daughter, then talked the daughter into letting her have them to give to Mama so she would have something. She never was sure about it, but was so grateful and will never forget her kindness. She isn't sure exactly how long she stayed with Sallie. It just so happens that Doris and Nell had bought the house that Mama's daddy had started to build. They were excited about living in the city. As it turned out, Mama did get to live a while in the "city house."

While Mama was going through all this, my daddy, Bennie, was on the ship going over to fight when they got the news that a peace treaty had been signed. What a great celebration they had on that ship. However, they were sent on to the Philippines, where he was stationed during the occupation after the war. Daddy had worked at Sears in their shipping department before he was drafted. This was a great advantage to him all his life. While in the army, they knew that he had training in shipping, so they put him on that detail while in the Philippines. Their job was to clean up after the war and send the equipment, supplies, etc. back to the United States. He made it to the rank of sergeant, commander of a squad.

Mama asked her daddy what he thought of her marrying Bennie. He was sitting by the fire, chewing his tobacco, and thinking. He thought and thought. He was studying this thing over. Finally, all he said was, "I just don't know about that boy."

1946

Mama and Daddy were married in Roswell, Georgia, on November 8, 1946. Mama took a paper grocery sack and put all her things in it. Her brother Charles stood on the back porch of the house protesting her decision, telling Mama she couldn't go. I am sure Mama had a hard time leaving, as had her sisters and brother before her. Jerry was seventeen and Charles was fourteen. Now it was her turn to find out what was out there in that whole new world. They went to the Methodist minister on Mimosa Boulevard and were married in the parsonage next to the church. It is still there today and is a very special place to Mama. Every time we pass there she says, "There's the house where we were married." John Albert and Daddy's sister, Nancy, "stood" with them. They drove back to Atlanta to tell Daddy's parents that they were married and then back up to Roswell to tell Mama's sister, Grace. Grace invited them to stay there for the night, which they did. Aunt Grace lived on a farm on Holcomb Bridge Road, and today the Red Lobster restaurant is there. For many years Mama and Daddy would go there on their anniversary. They were married on Friday and fixed their apartment on Saturday, then on Sunday rode up to Tallulah Gorge in north Georgia for the day. They counted that as their honeymoon.

Mama's in-laws cleaned out the basement of their house for them. They spent the day after they got married buying furniture for their one-room basement apartment. They got a bedroom suite and a table and four chairs to furnish their new home. Daddy had already started buying the lot next door to his parents. When he was young, Daddy would give any money he made to his father for safekeeping, then Pop-Paw gave it back to him as needed. Pop-Paw would make payments on the property next door for Daddy because Daddy was not old enough to buy it in his own name. Later, while he was in the army, he would send money to his father, who would make payments for him. "The government sent Pop-Paw and Mom-Maw House one hundred and ten dollars a month out of Daddy's pay."

After they got married, Mama and Daddy both worked at Sears at 675 Ponce De Leon Avenue, Atlanta, Georgia. I recently learned that that Sears building is a shopping mall called Ponce Market. Mama and Daddy took their paychecks every week and bought material to build their house. They worked all day then came home in the evenings and worked on their new house, building it themselves. Granddaddy Morris provided some lumber for the house.

They had just gotten the house to a point where they could live there, and Mama thought she would cook some butterbeans in a pressure cooker. Since she had never used one before, this was a brave decision. Sure enough, while they were busy working in another room, they heard a loud noise.

Running to the kitchen, they found their dinner all over the room—and in the rafters too!

Mama told me they had just finished tiling the floor in the kitchen, and as Daddy was painting, somehow, he dropped the can full of paint. It landed straight up, but splattered paint all in Daddy's face. Mama wanted to laugh but thought better of it as she helped him clean the paint out of his eyes.

1948

On November 25, 1948, I came into the world, and 1859 Claremont Street was my first home too. The year I was born Daddy went to work for the Ruralist Press. It was a printing company, and they printed the telephone books for the whole southeast. Naturally, Daddy was in shipping, and eventually worked his way up in the company to management. He was over the whole shipping department. Daddy worked for them forty-three years, and when he retired, they put his picture on the front of the Atlanta, Georgia, telephone book. They made a few special copies of it just for Daddy to have and share with family.

When I was just a baby, Mama and Daddy were baptized together at DeFoor Avenue Baptist Church. They joined that church, but the church didn't have a baptismal pool, Mama told me, so they had the baptism at another church. Helen McKinney held me while they were baptized. Mama said Daddy had received Christ when he was twelve at the church in Brookhaven where his family attended. Neither one of them had been baptized, though. What a special blessing to share. Mama told me just today about a group from DeFoor Avenue Baptist Church that came to her house for a weekly prayer meeting.

When Mama was pregnant with me, she went to stay with Bernice's boys, Walter, Robert, and Mickey, for a week while Bernice went to see her husband, Al, who was working in Tennessee. It was a hard week, but she enjoyed the boys. When she came home, Bernice brought two maternity dresses for Mama. One was blue and pink and one was all blue.

After Mama left home to get married and moved to Atlanta, Jerry, Charles, and Granddaddy moved again. Instead of building a house this time, Granddaddy moved a little house from the end of Wooten Road to the right of the big house that Mama loved, the last home Mama knew before she got married.

1951

Grandma Power passed away on January 21, 1951. She had cancer and died in her house on Power's Ferry Road. I only saw her a few times and don't really remember her, but I do remember playing in her front yard there on Power's Ferry Road near the river. I can see a white house on a high hill and big oak trees in the front yard. She was a remarkable woman who survived so much heartache and hardships. She was a woman of faith, though, and that got her through. Mama remembers how she canned vegetables that she grew herself and sold them in Atlanta. Mama told me she had an old surrey and she let the grandchildren play with it. One would be the horse and the other would ride, taking turns.

They called it Backbone Ridge. They would walk up one side of it and down the other side to get to Grandma's house. As Mama was remembering that path to Grandma's—where

they picked blueberries, honeysuckle, and sweet shrubs—
she suddenly remembered a special day in her life.

"I had gone over to Grandma's house, and she gave me
the portrait of my mother—the one that was hanging in her
house, the one that she treasured. Grandma wrapped it
carefully in a quilt, and I carried it back over Backbone Ridge
and down the other side to my house. The portrait was taken
when my mother was around twenty-two. She had had
typhoid fever and was weak, but she was able to sit up in
bed. They dressed her and took her picture." That portrait
still hangs in Mama's bedroom today.

Ethel moved into the big Wooten Road house after Paul
was born on April 28, 1951. She and Ruse Moss had seven
children. Paul was the youngest. When he was born, Ethel
and Paul came to stay with Mama and Daddy at their house
on Claremont Street in Atlanta, for about a week. Jimmy and
Jayne stayed with Mama's sister, Sallie. Sidney, Irma, Jo, and
Nita were at home in Newtown. Ethel and her children lived
in the house on Wooten Road for many years.

My granddaddy married for a third time on June 23, 1951,
and moved into Annie Elizabeth (Lizzy) Campbell's house
on Eves Road, as it is called now. This meant leaving Jerry
and Charles at home to take their turn at housekeeping.
Charles was still in high school, and he had to milk the cow,
cook, etc. "Jerry was working for Mr. Early. He thought a lot
of Jerry," Mama said. Ethel would come out to the little
house and make sure they got up in time for work and
school. Mama recalls that "Daddy bought Charles and Jerry
a ringer-type washing machine after she left home."

Ethel lived on that property for almost all her life. She
bought two acres plus the little house where Granddaddy,

Charles, and Jerry had lived. She worked very hard to save enough money to build a new house. She was an amazing woman. She was so well thought of at her church, where she kept the nursery for many years. I loved to hear her laugh.

1952

Then three years, one month, and twelve days after I was born, on January 6,1952, my brother, Bennie Lee House Jr., was born. I went to stay with Mama's sister, Grace, in Roswell. I can remember standing in the baby bed at night crying for Mama. Later, back at home, I told a neighbor, while sitting on the steps at the back of our house, that "he cried a lot." Mama loved to tell that story.

The same year that Lee was born, 1952, Mama's brother Charles, at age twenty, was drafted into the army. He was sent to Korea and served as an MP (Military Police). When he came home, he lived with Mama and Daddy for a while.

1956

In 1956 we were so happy to be moving into a brand-new house! 374 Norcross Street, Roswell, Georgia, was our address. Q. S. King was the builder. Funny what you remember. I remember looking back at Howell Mill Elementary School as we drove away for the last time, wondering about this new adventure awaiting us in the country town of Roswell. We were sad to leave Mom-Maw and Pop-Paw. It was an hour's drive from Atlanta to Roswell back then. Having lived all my life next door to them, I would miss them terribly.

Mama loved visiting with the neighbors on Norcross Street. The Smith family lived next door to us on one side, and the Cagles lived on the other side of our house. Grace, Mama's first cousin and her husband, Garlon Collett, lived two doors down. Next to them were the Christophers. John and Lou Taylor lived behind us on Afton Drive, as did Coach Smith and his family and the Parks family. The Taylors invited us to Roswell Second Baptist Church. Lee and I knew their daughters, Connie and Shelia, at school. Growing up at that church laid a foundation for our faith, and we will be forever grateful.

When Mama and Daddy moved from Atlanta to Roswell, they took all their love letters they had written during the war, read them to each other, laughed, and burned them. One day at church, Mama ran into her old mailman, Mr. DeLong. He told her, "I used to bring you those letters from Bennie during the war." Oh, how we would love to have those letters today!

It was spring break when we moved from Atlanta to Roswell. The very same week we moved, Mama's sister's house burned to the ground! They were burning some paper and a piece landed on the roof. Of course, word got out and we all went over there. They tried to save some things, but really all was lost. Everyone was safe, though. Aunt Grace had been over at the new house helping Mama wax the floors before they moved the furniture in. Aunt Grace, Frances, Margaret, and W. G. went to Aunt Lelia and Uncle Wesley's the first night, then came and stayed with us. Uncle Walter was traveling in his work. Our new house was small, but we managed. Mama's family all pitched in to help. Mama cooked and took food over to the men in the family who were working on the garage apartment that soon became their temporary home while a new house was built.

We have so many amazing cousins. Ethel and Ruse Moss were married and have Sidney, Irma, Jo, Nita, Jimmy, Jayne, and Paul. Bernice and Al have five children: Walter, Robert, Mickey, Rita, and Renee. Grace and Walter have three children: Frances, who died at age nineteen in a car accident, Margaret, and W. G. Jr. (Walt). Sallie and Neal have three children: Thomas, Lynda, and Ellen. Genie and Virgil have two children: Joe and Danny.

I must tell you this about my mama's brothers. They all married Bettys. We refer to them as Fred's Betty, Jerry's Betty, and Charles's Betty. Fred and Betty Duprie were married and have four children: Freddie, Gary, Perry, and Robin Ann. Jerry and Betty Bowen were married on December 3, 1954, and have three children: Sandra, Marcia, and Jerry Jr. Charles and Betty Warbington were married on June 2, 1956, and have three children: David, Connie, and Ricky.

Mama's siblings never treated nor thought of each other as anything but full brothers and sisters. As a matter of fact, Mama and her sisters, who lived in and around Atlanta, got together once a month to have what they called their "spend the day." This went on for years. They took turns having the others over for lunch and to spend the better portion of the day together. They all loved flowers and brought plants or cuttings to give to the ones who wanted them. If they were working on a new quilt, as so often Aunt Grace was, they would bring pieces to show. They cooked, crocheted, knit, sewed, and made crafts. One time they were into making jackets out of old jeans. They would share their crafts, plants, vegetables, or whatever they had with each other. They were close and relied on each other. Even Genie, who lived in

Iowa, would send letters to be shared, with maybe a clipping out of her local paper about the things that would interest them. If there was any family news from Iowa, Texas, or from Jerry or Charles's family (two of the Bettys worked, and Fred's Betty lived in Texas), that was shared as well.

1914: Luther Burney Morris and Eugenia Power Morris

Family of Samuel Adam Power
and Margaret Samantha Spruill Power
Back row: *Eugenia, Ruby, Fannie Lou*
Front row: *Samantha and Samuel, Alice in her lap, and Wesley*
and Lillian standing

Power Girls: Eugenia (back), Ruby (left),
and Fannie Lou (right)

Lillian Power at the World's Fair 1913, Knoxville, TN
Back row: *Elmer Whit, Lillian Power, Mamie White, Nettie*
Smith, and Edith Power.
One not named on back of original picture.

*Mary Lillian Power,
age twenty-two*

*1915: Mary Lillian
Power's diploma from
Crossroads School*

Artwork by Mary Lillian Power

Artwork by Mary Lillian Power

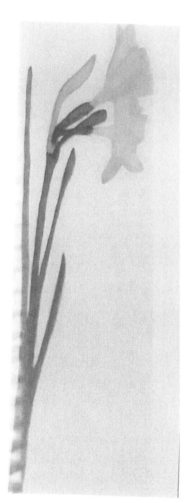

*Artwork by Mary
Lillian Power*

Cross Roads School.
Lillian Power. Language 7th gr.

1. (The) Lord is (my) shepherd,
I shall (not) want.
He maketh me [to lie
down] [in green pastures]
he leadeth me [besid
the still waters.]

2. [At last] (the) angel stopped
[at a low cottage] and
opened (the) door [into a
poor, cheerless room.]

Cross Roads School.
Lillian Power.   7th gr.

My Garden 60' by 60'.

Onions Feb. 15	Beans May 18.
Onions Feb. 15	Beans May 18
English peas Feb 15	Cabbage June 12
Tomatoes May.	Turnips Aug.
Walk.	Walk.
Early cucumbers. March.	Onions Nov.
Sweet peppers Apr.	Okra June.
Lettuce Feb.	Cantaloupes. Apr.
Early beans March	Cantaloupe June.
Onions Dec.	Onions Dec.

Samples of schoolwork done at Crossroads School in 1915

House of Samuel Wesley Power

"The Old Morris Place," built 1895, on Mid-Broadwell Road in Alpharetta, Georgia, is Granddaddy Morris's childhood home, and is still standing today

Lillian Power (left)
and unknown friend

Luther Burney Morris working for the county, hauling water

1913: Glen and Luther Morris at the Roswell Square on their wagon carrying hay and corn

Mama at age nine at Hammond School

*Mama at age ten at
Hammond School*

*1946: Mama in
Atlanta, soldier
not known*

Katherine Morris, age seventeen

Sergeant Bennie Lee House

1945:
Katherine and Nancy
House, Bennie's sister

1945:
Katherine Morris

*1946:
Bennie and
Katherine,
dating picture*

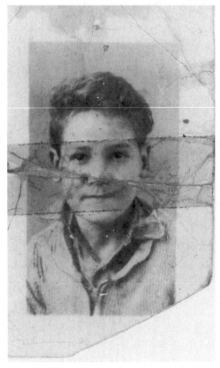

*Bennie Lee House,
age six*

Mama's house on Wooten Road

Roswell Methodist Church Parsonage on Mimosa Boulevard

November 1946:
Newlyweds Bennie and Katherine at Chastain Park

The sawmill

Easter 1947:
Jerry, Katherine, and Charles, house on Wooten Road

1949: Bennie, Katherine, and Joyce

1951:
Mama and me

1952: Joyce, Mama, Daddy, and Lee

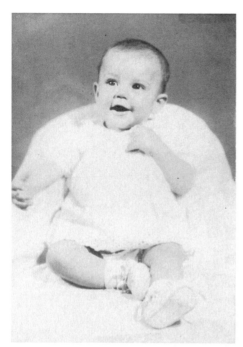

1949:
Vivian Joyce

1952:
Bennie Lee House Jr.

1958:
Lee, Anna,
and Joyce

1960:
Anna,
Joyce,
and Lee

Houses Celebrate 40th Anniversary

Katherine and Bennie House celebrated their 40th Wedding Anniversary on November 8, 1986, at the Fellowship Bible Church in Roswell. They have lived in the Alpharetta - Roswell area for over 30 years.

1986: Mama and Daddy at Fellowship Bible Church celebrating their fortieth wedding anniversary

Southern Bell®
A *BELL*SOUTH Company

New!
Effective May 16, 1992
Area Code 706

Still Making
B.L. "BENNIE" HOUSE cations
History
see page 2

43 YRS. SERVICE

Greater Atlanta

100% Recyclable

RESIDENCE

April 1992

1992: Telephone book cover recognizing Daddy's retirement after forty-three years at the Ruralist Press

1996: Bennie and Katherine celebrating their fiftieth wedding anniversary at the Polo Fields Golf and Country Club

*2006: Celebrating their sixtieth wedding anniversary and Bennie's
eightieth birthday at Young Deer Park on Lake Lanier
Left to right: Lee, Jan, Jessica, Jonathan, Jacque, Jennifer,
Chris, Nannie, Granddaddy, Joy, Joe,
Brittany, Jeff, and Donna
Front row: Coleman, Michael, Sarah, Gillian,
Hunter, and Taylor*

2016: Christmas with the family
***Back row:** Jonathan, Joy, Gillian, Michael,*
Coleman, Taylor, and Chris
***Second row:** Jessica, Jacque, Jennifer, Sarah,*
Joe, Brittany, Hunter, Donna, and Jeff
***Front row:** Lee, Jan, Cameron, Lola, Harrison,*
and Nannie (Katherine)

Chapter 6
Almost the Rest of the Story

Train up a child in the way he
should go, even when he is old he
will not depart from it.
—Proverbs 22:6 (NASB)

Mama was a homemaker, but at different times she worked at other jobs. She kept neighborhood children after school, Anna Smith, for one, who became like a sister. There were others. She would go to work with Daddy sometimes when they needed help running a large telephone book, like Miami or Atlanta. She worked at Kindercare Daycare for a while and Kmart. One job was helping in the cafeteria at Haynes Bridge Middle School in Alpharetta, North Roswell Elementary, and later at Northwestern Elementary School in Crabapple. Mama and Daddy both were hard workers and knew how to stretch a dollar.

My childhood was perfect. Mama and Daddy loved each other. We were in church twice on Sunday and Wednesday-night prayer meeting. Daddy was a student of the Word. He was one of the first to tape sermons and take to those who were homebound. He would teach a Sunday school lesson, and then play the sermon for them. We had everything we needed and more. Our home life would be characterized as the typical middle class of the fifties and sixties—Small Town USA.

1959

One Sunday morning, when I was ten years old, we went back to DeFoor Avenue Baptist Church in Atlanta. The preacher preached, but I cannot tell you a thing he said. There was tugging at my heart by the Holy Spirit. I looked up at Mama and asked, "Can I go?" as the altar call was given. I knelt and prayed, "Lord, save me! Lord save me!" And He did. That is the most precious place in my memory and in my heart. I immediately had a hunger for the Word and the desire to tell people what He had done. The first hymn I learned was taught to me by Mama, "Sweet Hour of Prayer," by W. W. Walford. It is still one of my very favorites. I urge you to read through all the verses. I remember saying to my little brother, Lee, who was just six at the time, "Pick a number from one to one hundred fifty," and I would read the Psalm he chose. Some years later, he, too, would go forward, after a sermon by Berry Henderson, at Roswell Second Baptist Church. I remember seeing him "slide in at home plate" as he prayed to receive Christ as his personal Lord and Savior. He is a testimony to the Lord every day of his life. He is a very precious, patient, kind, loving man with a great sense of humor.

1967

My wedding to Joseph Lamar McDonald took place on June 11, 1967. We started our married life in Baytown, Texas. After I was married, Mama and Daddy moved their membership to Lebanon Baptist Church, where Mama sang in the choir and helped with Vacation Bible School and many other church events.

1974

Lee married Jan Strickland on June 15, 1974, at the Roswell First Baptist Church.

Then, in 1975, a tragic event occurred that changed the course of our lives. I had been married to Joe McDonald for eight years, and we had two children, Donna, almost six, and Jody, three. My husband, Joe, graduated from Georgia Tech and was in central engineering with Gulf Oil. He was out at the Cedar Bayou Olefin Plant in Baytown, Texas, working during "shutdown" (that's when they turn off everything and make repairs). There was an accident, and he was killed along with another electrical engineer. My precious husband, just thirty-one, was called home by his Creator. I know where he is. He told me his favorite verse in the Bible was John 3:16, because as he put it, "It says it all in a nutshell." Joe McDonald Sr. was kind, loving, handsome, and intelligent. He was a Christian man, with a smile that would light up any room and any heart. The loss was great, and those were difficult days. But Jesus had "cut covenant" with a little ten-year-old girl. He kept all His promises, the ones I knew and the ones I was yet to learn. The Rock was firm. Mama, Daddy, and my brother, Lee, flew out to Humble, Texas, to be with us. It was hard, but God is faithful.

Now we come to where my story begins, but that's for another time. Let me say this, though. Back in Georgia, the family I have been writing about was all there—to hold my hand, to encourage me to eat, and to take care of this young widow and her children. Mama, Daddy, Lee, Jan, Dorcas and Rucker McDonald (Joe's parents), Joe's brother, Rucker and his wife, Carol, and their children, Terra and Tonya, were grieving too. They all supported us in every way—

great and small. The church family supported us as well. Joe and I were both raised in Roswell, and the members of First Baptist Church, Second Baptist Church, and Lebanon Baptist Church were all there to walk through this valley with us. My heart is still so filled with love and gratitude to those dear friends. As I reflect on all this, I think of Berry and Betty Henderson, Dick and Carol Hester, and Brantley and Elnora Seymour, pastors of those churches, and their wives, who were there as well, ministering to this hurting family. You will never be forgotten—your encouragement and prayers got us through.

Joe died on the Fourth of July, and my brother and his wife, Jan, were expecting their first child in October. We were at the same time experiencing joy and pain. A new life was coming, but it was also overshadowed by death. However, on the sixteenth of October, Christopher Lee House was born, and he brought great joy that was much needed to our family. Mama and Daddy's third grandchild would be joined later by sister, Jennifer, December 9, 1976, and brother, Jonathan, on May 14, 1979.

1976

Granddaddy Morris (Luther Burney Morris) enjoyed his later years staying with each of his children, taking turns a month at a time. Eventually he did live in the Canton Nursing Home, and one day he went to lunch, and then came back to his room to rest in his chair. A little later he was found sitting in his chair. He died peacefully on September 21, 1976, at age eighty-four. He joined his first two wives and his two infant sons in heaven. Their graves are in the Methodist Church Cemetery on Mount Vernon

Road in Sandy Springs, Georgia, next to Arlington Cemetery. You can find many of the Power and Morris family plots in this cemetery.

1977

Mama, Jerry, and Charles decided to sell their property that they had inherited from their mother, Lillian. It was sold in March of 1977. Some of it went into a subdivision and some of it was made into a national recreation area.

1978

Mama and Daddy sold the home on Norcross Street. They found some beautiful, wooded acreage in Alpharetta, Georgia. My brother, Lee, who was a builder, built their home there. They both loved gardening, and their home and yards were beautiful. It was called "Dogwood Hill."

1979

Mama, Daddy, and I were privileged to sign the charter committing to start a church. Even before that, Charlie Lindsey, Norm Smith, and Bob White had met for two years on Tuesday mornings with Dan DeHaan in his office to pray for God to move in the Roswell area. As Annette Lindsey recalls, "They prayed down on their faces, seeking God's guidance." Then Walk Thru the Bible moved its headquarters from Portland, Oregon, to Atlanta. Joe Usry, Art Vander Veen, and Bob Roland were with WTB and had held seminars at First Baptist Church in Atlanta. The Lord brought these men together. The men from Roswell had been talking with Dr. Stanley about wanting to start a church in the Roswell area. Joe Usry, who was the assistant pastor at that time to Dr. Stanley, was asked to be one of the pastors of this new church, along with Art and Bob.

The Whites, the Lindseys, the Smiths, the DeHaans, my family, Mama, and Daddy—along with many other families—had been meeting in the Human Resource Center on Oak Street in Roswell on Sunday evenings during the summer of 1979. By the end of the summer, it seemed that the interest was great enough to start putting together a plan for this new church. Don and Susie Newby led the music, and Dan or Joe would teach. Then, in September, the group decided to meet in Charlie and Shirley Morgan's basement for four Sunday evenings. Bob Roland recalls how the furnace kept cutting on and off during these meetings. Nothing could dampen our spirits, though. We were such a happy, excited group. The meetings were to explain and lay out for the group the plan for the new church, its philosophy, ministry, role of the elders and deacons, children's ministry, etc. Then on the fourth of those meetings—explaining what was involved in this endeavor—a charter or covenant was presented. With much soul searching and prayer, sixty-one people committed to this new adventure with God. Dan DeHaan, Joe Usry, Bob White, Charlie Morgan, Norm Smith, and Charley Lindsey, along with Art and Bob, were a few of the men God called to undertake this task. They explained that this was a serious commitment. We felt led by God to sign that simple piece of paper that meant so much.

The first official church worship service was on October 7, 1979, at Mimosa Elementary School. Joe was the first full-time pastor, and Myles Lorenzen came in December. Art and Bob were both part time, though. Roy Ludwig was the chairman of the board of elders. Art came on full time the next year, 1980, and Bob the next year, 1981. We remember Bob and Marlene White, Norm and Dixie Smith, Dan and Penny DeHaan, Joe and Rosemary Usry, Charley and Annette Lindsey, John and Betty Queen, Al and Bobbie Blackburn, Roy and Nell Ludwig, Charlie and Shirley Morgan, Mary Kay Stallings, Woots and Sarah Caines, Tim Ake, Carol Freeman, Mike Morris, Craig Morris, Mike Sanders, Ted and Lucia Whitfield, and Cindy Brannon, along with Mama and Daddy and me, as some of the first families. It was a wonderful day! Susie Newby and Don, with his guitar, led the singing. They also led the youth group. Don and Susie had plans to go to Germany all along, and we knew they were here for just a short while. They were our first missionaries. They still serve there today. Darien Cooper was our first women's fellowship director. Our first baptism was a real event. They brought in a brand-new septic tank from Cliff Wagner's business, and Paul Ryzek was covered in concrete dust when he came out of the water. We met in Mimosa Elementary School for four and a half years. The need to find another place to meet was answered by the Roswell Roller Skating Rink. Those were exciting times in our lives and in the life of FBC.

Mama was always involved in the women's ministry. She was on the refreshment committee early in the life of the church. She did a lot of calling and encouraging. We all had to take our turn in the Learning Center. That was what we called the children's ministry. Mama and Daddy worked together in the different classes, nursery on up. You really got to know your team when you worked in the Learning Center. There were so few of us that we all had to pitch in all the time. We were of the same mind in basic Bible doctrine. We could fellowship around the Word, hence the name Fellowship Bible Church. Our Sunday school classes were called Fellowships. In those early days, we decided to have a meeting once a month on Sunday nights in different homes. I remember the very first mini-church, as we called them, was in my home. We were determined that church meetings, etc. would not interfere with everyone's home life and the needs of their families. We believed in the plurality of leadership, so the whole burden of pastoring would not fall on one man. My daddy was there every Sunday to help set up and take down chairs and equipment, as we were not in our own building yet. He had such a servant's heart.

I remember the Sunday we had the groundbreaking ceremony and service at the property we had just purchased. Nineteen acres, and God did it! We sat on tree stumps and babies slept in cars with the doors open not far away.

1986

On February 1, 1986, Mike and Debbie McCrum and their family came to Fellowship, and Mike took over as youth pastor.

In August 1986, we had the first meeting in our new church building, at 480 West Crossville Road, Roswell, Georgia. The elders took twelve large rocks to place as a memorial to all that God had done. The monument is still there in front of the church today. In the foyer of the church is a piece of artwork made with wood from the original front doors of the church. It is beautiful.

Mama and Daddy celebrated their fortieth wedding

anniversary in the new church building in November 1986. It was the first special event held at Fellowship Bible Church. The walls were just concrete blocks, and we had to bring in wooden lattice screens to decorate as a background for the cake table. As a church, we were so excited to have our own place. This year we celebrate thirty-nine years since that first official church worship service. To God be the glory.

1996

In the fall of 1996, I helped open the new elementary school at the end of Wooten Road in Roswell. Each day, for seventeen years, I drove past the land that had belonged to my mama's family in the 1940s. The road was their driveway back then. My cousin Jimmy still owns some land there. Memories would flood my mind of those days gone by when we had Granddaddy's birthday dinners under the big oak tree. A new school, Northwood, on old land. It felt like home.

We celebrated Mama and Daddy's fiftieth anniversary on November 8, 1996, at the Polo Fields Country Club. Vince Collins sang one of Mama's favorite songs, "Find Us Faithful," written by Steve Green, 1988. Bob Roland led us in a prayer of thankfulness for Mama and Daddy and the Lord's faithfulness to them. It was a grand affair.

2000

Because of some health issues, Mama and Daddy moved again, not far from Dogwood Hill, to a smaller place with less steps. It, too, was beautiful with the evidence of their love for gardening. Daddy could root any plant. There are many people who still talk about his plants, and some refer to one of the trees he rooted and gave to so many as "Bennie's Trees."

In 2006, we celebrated Mama and Daddy's sixtieth wedding anniversary and Daddy's eightieth birthday with family at one of Daddy's favorite fishing spots on Lake Lanier.

Mama and Daddy hosted Bible studies in their home with Tom Grady. Later, also, Mama held a women's Bible study in the daytime for older women that met weekly. The women of the church fixed food every year for the Missions Conference. We all worked hard on the first playground. There are so many stories we could tell. The Fellowship Christian School came later. FBC is still going strong today. We had our rough times too, but God has been so faithful. We are so thankful for Crawford and Karen Loritts and their ministry.

2008

Mama and Daddy were faithful members of the Trailblazers Fellowship Group until Daddy went to be with the Lord in May 2008 after a nine-month struggle with lung cancer. What a strong, faithful believer he was. We couldn't imagine our world with him not in it. Mama still attends Trailblazers when she is able. Bob Roland, Tim McDaniel, and Larry Goar spoke at Daddy's service and Verna Law sang. Thirteen years before, Bob Roland so wonderfully preached my Daddy's father's funeral, in 1995.

2018

Those two, young people in 1946 (she was eighteen and he was twenty) fell in love, got married, worked hard to provide for their family, and served the Lord as best as they knew how. Mama just turned ninety. I have been able to ask her questions to make this account accurate to the best of her memory. I feel as though I have gone back in time and met my great-great-great-grandparents and generations that followed. I hope you enjoy getting to know them and getting to know what it was like for a little girl and her family as they worked to make it through those Depression years. There is a great testimony here to strong people with a strong faith and a big God who protected them and allowed them to survive.

Epilogue
Still Not the Rest of the Story

Remembering what God has done in
our past gives us greater faith for
what He's doing in our present.
—Jon Jorgenson

There are so many stories still untold. Mama is a great storyteller. Just when I think the book is finished, Mama will remember something, and I think, "Where does that fit in the story?" Like the time she and Daddy played Mary and Joseph in the church Christmas program at Defoor Avenue Baptist Church. That was not long after they married and before I came along. Or like the fact that her daddy was there at the revival meeting the night she accepted Christ, and she remembers they sang the song "The Good Old Gospel Ship." Or the fact that the first time she saw anyone make fried pies was at Mrs. Thomason's house. She would take them to the workers at the sawmill where her husband worked with Mama's daddy. Or the time she had permission to go home with "the little Wright girl." She lived not too far from the school. When they got home, her mother gave them cornbread and milk for their after-school snack. Then they went back to Hammond School because Santa Claus was going to be there. She got lots of presents but can't remember what they were. When she got home, her sister, Ethel, said to hide them so Santa would leave more. Santa did leave more.

Something triggered Mama's memory again, and she

said, "Oh yeah, there is something I have been meaning to tell you. Remember I told you about when they paved Power's Ferry? What I didn't tell you was that they dug a big drainage ditch next to the road. They filled that ditch with huge rocks. We worked our way through those rocks making a path to Grandma's. Some years later, crabapple trees grew up through those rocks. They were the biggest and best crabapples!" She relayed this information as if it were so special.

We just celebrated Mama's ninetieth birthday. It was a wonderful time of reunion with old friends and family. We had a reception at church a week before the actual day and then a party at Lee and Jan's house on the day, April 28. We were overwhelmed with gratitude for all who came to see Mama. Mama told me that the cake that day was so beautiful. Later, after the party was over, Mama told me that she had never had a birthday cake until her children were big enough to make sure she had one. I never knew this until now. After all the cakes she has made for us and others, to think, she didn't have that one thing that we all take for granted on her special day. She had two big ones this year!

Mama told me she has had a lot of different names over the years. Her daddy called her "Kap"; her husband called her "Kat"; her children call her Mama, Mother, Mom. Grandkids call her Nannie, except for Donna and Jonathan; they call her "Nan." One of my friends called her Kathy. She is a great-grandmother, and her great-grands call her Nannie too, but she told me she always knew she would be "great" one day. She loves all these people and loves her different names, but there is another name she likes to be called, and that is Christian, a child of God. This is what Mama told me.

So let me say this has just been a glimpse into her life and the lives of those around her. There are so many moments, days, years that are not recorded. She lived and is still living her story at age ninety. Just like the rest of us, days went by and turned into years, and they make up a lifetime. These are the things Mama told me. These are the things she remembers. Mama loves her family. She and Daddy have two children, five grandchildren, and nine great-grandchildren. Mama and Daddy's legacy will not be of a financial nature, although they did well in that respect. Their legacy will be their Christian faith, which they have passed down to their children and grandchildren. Faith in the one true God who knows we long to know Him, so He sent His Son as an ambassador, Jesus Christ, to earth so we could know Him and accept His gift of forgiveness and eternal life. She has always and will always worry about and pray for her family and friends. She has faith that God will take care of them and they in turn will trust Him with grateful hearts for all He has done. She looks forward to seeing her husband again, along with her sisters, brothers, parents, and all those who have gone on before her. Heaven is on her mind, and she spends much of her day reading her Bible. A dream about Daddy makes her so happy. Heaven is a real place, and Jesus is the door (John 10). Mama's faith in Jesus and His sacrifice of His own life to cover mankind's sin is a gift she has already received. The story doesn't end on this earth. The rest of the story takes place in Heaven. It never ends, because she will go on living for all eternity. Both Mama and I hope to see you there.

Testimony

by Katherine Morris House
April 6, 2010
**Inspired by an article by a pastor
called "Great Comebacks"**

Just as Jesus overcame, we too can be overcomers. The crucified Savior became the risen LORD.

I was born the ninth child of a family of eleven children. I have had to overcome a lot of things. My father had to overcome a lot before I was ever born. He married a girl he truly loved in 1914. They had seven children. When the seventh child was eight days old, his wife died. Two weeks later, his two-year-old son died. He overcame that, and married his wife's sister, my mother. They had a child and he died, another son. They had three more children. Seven years later his wife had a mental breakdown and was institutionalized. With nine children, one of which was me age four, all the children were placed in an aunt's or uncle's home, except the three youngest. I, being the oldest of those three, was placed in a foster home, then in a children's home. Finally, I did go to my Aunt Grace's. By then the oldest daughter was twenty and able to look after the younger ones, so my father gathered all his children back together and we moved back to Sandy Springs. We had a lot to overcome. Everyone's life was different. One sister, Bernice, never came back. She loved Aunt Georgia Ann and Aunt Georgia Ann loved her. Genie lived with Uncle Ben and Aunt Pauline and loved them dearly. She would go back to visit often.

The hardest thing I had to overcome at that time was that everyone said their mother had died, but my mother was sick, in the hospital. In fact, she had a sickness that was frowned upon. So I just said my mother was dead too. I felt like I lived a lie until I was old enough to realize that God had a plan for my life. I would try to explain all the things I had to overcome, like changing schools almost every year. As each one of my brothers and sisters left home, either to take a job in Atlanta, or go in the military, or get married, that meant I had to take on more and more responsibility. I had to take care of the house, milk the cow, churn the butter, do all the cooking, and wash all the clothes at the age of thirteen. We moved a lot. We moved from Sandy Springs to Roswell and then back to Sandy Springs. When I was fourteen, my Aunt Lucy carried me to church and explained the plan of salvation to me, and I accepted Jesus Christ as my Savior. I realized Jesus innocently suffered death like us and for us. He knew what it was like for things to go wrong, that sorrow could be turned into joy, defeat into victory, that even death could be overcome.

When I was sixteen years old I met my husband, and we married in 1946. Bennie served in the military two years. We married shortly after he returned home. We have two beautiful children, Joy and Lee. We have five grandchildren, and now have nine great-grandchildren.

The hardest thing I have had to overcome was the loss of my great husband of sixty-two years. We suffered together for ten months, and he went to be with the Lord on May 7, 2008. I know where he is, and I will see him again someday. I am sure I will have to overcome more things in this life, but I know God loves me and has a plan for me still.

With God's help, I can overcome!

Katherine Morris House

James Power & 1st wife
b. 4/15/1796
d. 12/16/1870

Samuel Wesley Power m. Mary Ann Hopkins
b. 7/13/1830   b. 3/23/1828
d. 12/19/1916   d. 11/24/1908

Emma   Fannie   James   Alice   Elizabeth

Samuel
b. 9/5/1843 Adam m. Margaret Samantha Spruill
d. 12/1/1909 Power   b. 1/29/1875
                                  d. 1/21/1951

Grady

Wesley

William

Alice

Mary Lillian Power
b. 3/29/1899
d. 7/24/1971
2nd wife of
M. Luther Burney Morris

Eugenia Elizabeth Power
b. 10/15/1914
d. 4/14/1924 1st wife of
M. Luther Burney b. 4/14/1942
Morris d. 9/21/1976

Rudy   Fannie Lou

b. 4/26/1905
d. 4/22/2006
Ethel
m. Rose
Moss

b. 1/16/1917
d. 6/22/2005
Bernice
m. Al
Sewell

Sidney
Erma
Jo
Juanita
Jimmy
Jayne
Paul

b. 1/19/1919
d. 2/21/2002
Fred
m. Betty
Dupnic

Walter
Robert
Mickey
Rita
Renee

b. 4/18/1920
d. 3/27/1993
Grace
m. Walter
Shaw

Freddie
Gary
Perry
Robin Ann

b. 6/3/1921
d. 3/16/10
Sallie
m. Neal
Harper

Frances
Margaret
W.G.

b. 7/21/1923
d. 5/21/1924
L.B. Jr.

Lynda
Thomas
Ellen

b. 4/6/1924
d. 6/15/2014
Eugenia "Genie"
m. Virgil
Tilley

Joe
Danny

David
Hugh
b. 1926
d. 1927

b. 4/29/1928
Katherine
m. Bennie
House

Joyce
Lee

b. 10/14/1924
d. 11/20/2010
Jerry
m. Betty
Bowen

Sandra
Marcia
Jerry

b. 7/2/1932
Charles
m. Betty
Worthington

David
Connie
Ricky

Power Family Tree

JAMES POWER, b. 4/15/1790, d. 12/16/1870, and 1st wife had SAMUEL WESLEY POWER, b. 7/13/1830, d. 12/18/1916.

SAMUEL WESLEY POWER m. MARY ANN HOPKINS, b. 3/28/1828, d. 11/24/1908. They had Emma, Fannie, James, Alice, SAMUEL ADAM, and Elizabeth.

SAMUEL ADAM POWER, b. 9/1868, d. 12/1908, m. MARGARET SAMANTHA SPRUILL, b. 1/29/1875, d. 1/21/1951. They had EUGENIA ELIZABETH, b. 10/15/1894, d. 4/14/1924, Ruby, Fannie Lou, MARY LILLIAN, b. 3/29/1899, d. 7/26/1972, William, Wesley, Alice, and Grady.

EUGENIA ELIZABETH m. LUTHER BURNEY MORRIS, b. 4/14/1892, d. 9/21/1976. They had ETHEL IRENE, JANIE BERNICE, FRED BROOKS, GRACE MARGARET, SALLIE MAE, L. B. JR., and EUGENIA ELIZABETH (Genie).

MARY LILLIAN was the 2nd wife of LUTHER BURNEY MORRIS. They had DAVID HUGH, KATHERINE MARGENE, JERRY MYERS, and CHARLES EDWARD.

KATHERINE MORRIS, b. 4/28/1928, m. BENNIE LEE HOUSE, b. 10/31/1926, d. 5/7/2008. They had VIVIAN JOYCE, b. 11/25/1948, and BENNIE LEE HOUSE JR., b. 1/6/1952.

JOYCE HOUSE m. JOSEPH LAMAR MCDONALD, 6/11/1967. They had DONNA JOYCE MCDONALD, b. 7/25/1969, and JOSEPH LAMAR MCDONALD JR., b. 4/27/1972.

BENNIE LEE HOUSE m. JAN STRICKLAND, 6/15/1974. They had CHRISTOPHER LEE HOUSE, b. 10/16/1975, JENNIFER JAN HOUSE, b. 12/9/1976, and JONATHAN EDWIN HOUSE, b. 5/14/1979.

DONNA MCDONALD m. JEFFERY LYNN BAUMAN, 9/14/1991. They had twins TAYLOR LYNN BAUMAN and HUNTER JOSEPH BAUMAN, b. 5/6/1997.

JOSEPH MCDONALD m. BRITTANY KLEIN, 6/10/1995. They had SARAH JOSEPHINE MCDONALD, b. 3/25/1996, COLEMAN JOSEPH MCDONALD, b. 2/12/1998, MICHAEL JAMES MCDONALD, b. 6/10/2000, and GILLIAN JOYCE MCDONALD, b. 10/2/2002.

CHRISTOPHER LEE HOUSE m. JACQUE REAGLE, 5/27/2006. They had HARRISON WALTER HOUSE, b. 2/28/2008, and CAMERON LEE HOUSE, b. 6/21/2010.

JONATHAN EDWIN HOUSE m. JESSICA JAMROZY, 5/10/2003. They had LOLA GRACE HOUSE, b. 10/13/2009

*Charles at the Chattahoochee River, standing on a rock near where
the cabin was before the property was sold. Original property of
James Power and sons passed down to children.
Near where the ferry crossed.*

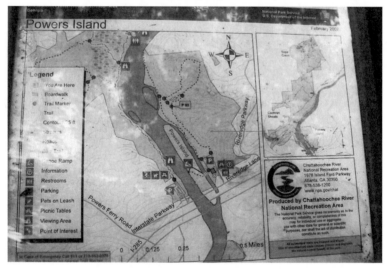

*Map of the Chattahoochee River National Recreation Area.
Built in 1978 after the Power property was sold.
Notice the name Power's Island.
Mama said they took the cow out there to graze.*

HISTORIC LANDMARK GONE

Only-Ashes, Chimney Ruins Remain of Old Power Home

By JIM BRADY

"Be it ever so humble,
There's no place like home."

How many times people have written and sung of the old southern homes can hardly be told, and in all likelihood tales of these places will continue to be spun until the end of time.

One of Georgia's disappearing landmarks in the War Between the States, the old Power home, located on Powers Ferry road, might be considered one of this section's most interesting and noteworthy. The final epic in the history of this old structure came two weeks ago—shortly before Christmas—when a fire broke out in one of the flues, and the house burned before firemen could prevent the tragedy.

Located nearly 14 miles from the center of metropolitan Atlanta, the Power home grew from an humble dwelling of a century ago into a proud structure, overlooking the muddy waters of the Chattahoochee river. It had been lived in for more than nine decades by descendants of the Power family.

For the past few years, though, the house had been lived in by several different families, the last of which were Mr. and Mrs. P. D. Christian Jr., who now live at 214 Fourteenth street, N. E.

Francis W. Clarke, who, before his death in 1938, was executive editor of The Constitution, at one time also lived in the Power house.

BUILT SIMPLE ABODE

Purchasing more than 300 acres of land of the fine Georgia countryside from the government—110 years ago—S. W. Power and his family established a farm and built the simple abode from logs and fastened them together with wooden pegs. Two massive chimneys were built at each end of the house facing each other. There the family lived for almost a century.

As the War Between the States neared Atlanta, living descendants of the family relate, there was nothing for the Power family to do but wait for the northern armies and pray that their home would be spared from fire. Then, in its fury, the war struck. Gen. Sherman's troops approached the banks of the Chattahoochee and built a bridge for his troops to cross.

So it was, that where S. W. Power operated a ferry enabling the country folk and the travelers to cross, Gen. Sherman constructed one of the first bridges in the neighborhood to span the Chattahoochee river.

Mrs. Margaret Samantha Power, widow of Samuel Adam Power, and 72-year-old granddaughter of S. W. Power, describes many of the exciting moments as told by her grandfather, as Sherman's men crossed the river and battled practically in her own front yard.

REACHED RIVER BANK

"At noon one day they reached the banks of the river," she said, "and by noon the next day they had that bridge built. After the battle was over, Sherman used our grounds and lawns as a headquarters while his men built a road through the hills. Although we feared the worst, we got off mighty easy when they finally moved on—all they took was a flock of our chickens and most of our stock."

A spry and congenial little old lady, Mrs. Power lived on the land that her grandfather bought for more than 50 years. She is active about her home on the other side of Power's Ferry road—opposite the smouldering ruins of her grandfather's proud creation.

The house itself sat atop a steep hill, and on all sides was surrounded by huge oak trees. Five fine oaks encircled the house and a long, winding driveway circled up the hill through well-kept grounds.

"It remained a three-room dwelling until about 40 years ago—when improvements were begun," Mrs. Power explained, "and as time went by, it was changed into a home that anyone would have been proud to have lived in."

Today, though, all that remains are the ruins and ashes—and memories of the happiness and tears of any old home. A living tribute to the family that first pioneered that section of Atlanta and ferried the early settlers of the wooded hills across the roaring waters of the Chattahoochee, greets the eyes of visitors as they ride or walk along Power's Ferry road. Look into the swirling waters of the Chattahoochee, along its banks and up on the hill where the two lonely chimneys stand—you will understand.

1946: Article in the paper about the Power's house burning

Aunt Nettie Power (wife of William Power)
and daughter, Marie Power Stewart.
Grandma Power's house on Power's Ferry Road.

January 12, 1949:
Grandma Power
(Samantha Spruill Power),
children not named

Children of Grandma (Margaret Samantha Spruill Power) and Grandpa Power (Samuel Adam Power): Wesley, William, Grady, Alice, Fannie Lou, and Ruby (Eugenia and Lillian not pictured)

*The Samuel Power family siblings, except Eugenia and
Lillian: Wesley, Fannie Lou, William, Alice, Grady, and Ruby*

*Made at the original spring or well that Sandy Springs is named
for, located across the street from the Methodist church and down
the hill, Mama told me.
Uncle Tom Jordan, Aunt Georgia Jordan, Aunt Grace Morris
Swofford (who later married William Davis), and
Elizabeth and Lorrine Swofford*

Sons of William Morris, Luther, the youngest, on the left

Family of William Morris
Back row: *Glenn, Vard, Ben, and Luther*
Front row: *Allie, Georgia, Grace, and Lucy*

*Mama and
Aunt Gillie Hamrick*

*Granddaddy
Morris with
Genie holding
Sidney*

1956: Family picnic at the cabin at Power's Ferry on the Chattahoochee River. Jayne, Nita, Frances, Jo, Ellen, Lynda, Margaret, Joyce, Lee, W. G., Sallie, and Neal in the background.

1956: Picnic at the river. Jimmy, Lee, Sallie, Thomas, Joe, Danny, and Virgil.

Luther Burney Morris

Christmas 1958:
Granddaddy
Morris,
Newtown
Community
Center

Luther Morris at
the Morris
Reunion at
North Fulton
Park (a.k.a.
Chastain Park)

*May 1962: Jayne, Ethel, Lee, Katherine, Nita, Joy,
and Granddaddy Morris*

*April 14, 1958: Granddaddy Morris's birthday dinner
at the house on Wooten Road.
David's birthday too!*

Brothers-in-law: Walter Stow, Virgil Tilley, Ruse Moss, Neal Harper, Bennie House, and Albert Stovall

1949: (All here but Fred) Katherine, Genie, Sallie, Grace, Bernice and Ethel, Charles, Granddaddy, and Jerry

*August 1971: Charles, Jerry, Katherine, Genie, Sallie,
Grace, Fred, Granddaddy, Bernice, and Ethel*

*Sallie, Katherine, Fred, Grace, Ethel, and Bernice.
Granddaddy and Jerry outside the Newtown
Community Center.*

The gang's all here: Katherine, Genie, Sallie, Grace, Bernice, Ethel, Charles, Jerry, and Fred

At the Morris Reunion: Charles, Fred, Bernice, Grace, Jerry, Ethel, Genie, Katherine, and Sallie

*Christmas 1983: Betty, Grace, Bernice, Ethel,
Katherine, and Sallie*

*2003: Jerry and Charles Morris with Sallie Morris Harper and
Bernice Morris Stovall at Katherine Morris House's seventy-fifth
birthday party*

June 2001: Sallie's eightieth birthday celebration
Back row: *Aubrey Morris, Jerry Morris, Fred Morris, and Charles Morris*
Front row: *Grace Morris Collett, Sallie Morris Harper, Katherine Morris House, and Bernice Morris Stovall*

February 4, 2007: Charles, Betty, Katherine, Bennie, and Sallie

On train trip from Atlanta to Chattanooga:
Ethel, Grace, and Mama

On train trip from Atlanta to Chattanooga:
Mama, Ethel, and Grace

1994:
Fred and Betty
Morris

1995:
Charles and
Betty Morris
at Martha's
Vineyard,
MA

2009:
Jerry and
Betty Morris

2016: Margaret Bruce Jordan, Charles Morris,
and Katherine Morris House

1944: Fred Brooks Morris

October 28, 1944: Genie and Virgil Tilley

1995: Virgil and Genie Tilley

November 1952:
Charles Morris

1953:
Charles and Jerry

*Graves of William Burney Morris and Charity Rhoda Morris.
Located at the Methodist Church Cemetery in Sandy Springs.*

*Graves of Luther Burney
Morris, first wife,
Eugenia, second wife,
Lillian, and two of their
children. Located at the
Methodist Church
Cemetery in Sandy
Springs.*

Graves of Samuel Wesley Power and Mary A. Power

Graves of Samuel Adam Power and Margaret Samantha Power

Cake at party

April 28, 2018: Katherine's ninetieth birthday, with grandson Joe, whose birthday was the day before

*Reception
at Fellowship
Bible Church*

Mama's Recipe File

I went through Mama's recipe file and found some of our favorite recipes. I tried also to include a recipe from each of Mama's sisters and other relatives. As I thought of the dishes I loved, but found nothing written down, I asked Mama to tell me how she made them. When credit is not given, it was Mama's recipe. I feel sure that generations to come will be glad to have these. Enjoy!

Main Dishes, Casseroles, Side Dishes, and Bread

Desserts

Main Dishes, Casseroles, Side Dishes, and Bread

ANGEL BISCUITS

- 5 c sifted self-rising flour
- 1/3 c sugar
- 1 c shortening
- 1 t soda
- 2 pkg yeast dissolved in 1/4 c lukewarm water
- 2 c buttermilk

Combine dry ingredients, cut in shortening, and stir in yeast and buttermilk.

Roll and cut as desired or make into Parker House rolls.

Bake on middle rack in oven at 450.

Dough may be covered and refrigerated as long as a week, using as needed.

AUNT BERNICE'S BBQ SAUCE

- 1/2 stick butter
- 1/2 onion, chopped
- 1/4 c brown sugar
- 1 T vinegar
- 1 c ketchup
- 1 T yellow mustard

Sauté the onion in butter then add remaining ingredients. Grill chicken until almost done then add the sauce and finish cooking.

BUTTERMILK BISCUITS

- 2 c self-rising flour
- 6 T Crisco
- 1 c buttermilk

I can't tell you how many times I have watched my mama make biscuits. She had a wooden dough tray that she kept in a big container that held her flour. She would get it out, add a little more flour, then with her hand get a little bit of Crisco and start working the dough by hand. When it was worked enough she would add a little buttermilk until it was the right consistency. Then, she would pinch off a little dough, roll it in a ball (with floured hands), place it in the greased pan, and press it down with her folded fingers (almost to a fist). Then they were ready to bake at 400 degrees for about 10 minutes.

***

In the kitchen Mama told me to
"save the butter wrapper to grease
the next pan."

***

ANNIE MAE'S BRUNSWICK STEW

- 1 can pork
- 1 can beef
- 1 can chicken or turkey
- 1 large onion, finely chopped
- 2 cans tomatoes
- 1 can creamed-style corn
- 1 can whole-kernel corn
- 1 bottle Bull's-Eye Original BBQ sauce

Combine all ingredients and cook for 1 1/2 to 2 hours in a slow cooker. Serve with crackers.

BUTTERMILK SALAD

- 1 small pkg Jell-O, orange (or your favorite)
- 1 c buttermilk
- 1/2 c pecans
- 1 small can crushed pineapple (do not drain)
- 4 oz Cool Whip

Mix pineapple and Jell-O together. Heat until dissolved.

Take off heat and add buttermilk. Pour into 8x11 casserole dish.

Refrigerate until partially set, about 30 minutes.

Fold in nuts and Cool Whip. Refrigerate until fully set.

This is one of our family favorites from the *Roswell First Baptist Cookbook.*

CHICKEN AND DUMPLINGS

- 4 chicken thighs, boneless and skinless
- 2 stalks of celery, cut up
- 1/2 large onion, cut into fourths
- 2 bouillon cubes

Stew chicken in water, celery, onion, and bouillon cube for about 45 minutes.

Take out, debone, and shred chicken with fork, and set aside.

Remove celery and onion from broth.

Dumplings:

Make the dough as if making a pie crust, but use cold water instead of milk.

Roll out very thin and cut into pieces about 2 inches long.

Add to boiling broth mixture.

Don't stir, just gently shake the pot.

They cook quickly.

Add chicken and heat a few minutes more.

***

When I said, "We're better than them,
aren't we, Mama?" Mama told me,
"Don't you ever let me hear you say that
we are better than anyone, young lady.
We are not!"

***

MAMA'S CHICKEN PIE

- chicken breasts
- chicken thighs
- celery
- onion
- bouillon cubes

Stew chicken in water.

Add some celery, bouillon cube, and onion to add flavor. (Amount of chicken and other ingredients varies according to how big you want your pie.)

Stew the chicken at least 45 minutes after it begins to boil. Next, boil 3–4 eggs.

After the chicken is done, take it out of the broth and allow to cool so you can debone it, or you can use boneless chicken.

While the chicken and eggs are cooling, make the crust.

Crust:

- 2 c of self-rising flour
- 1/2 c of Crisco
- 1/2 c of milk

Cut Crisco into flour. Add milk a little at a time while stirring until dough follows fork around in bowl. Add a little more milk if needed, not too much, though.

Grease the bottom and sides of a 13x9-inch pan.

Roll dough on floured surface and cut into strips.

Line the sides of the pan with dough.

Put a few strips of dough in the bottom and dot with butter.

Place cut-up, deboned chicken and chopped eggs in pan.

Pour broth over chicken to cover well.

Roll out dough for the top crust. (You can use canned biscuits.)

Cut into strips and cover chicken lattice style. Dot top with butter.

Bake at 375 degrees for 30–40 minutes OR until golden brown.

AUNT BETTY'S COLLARDS

- collards
- bacon grease, or drippings from a pot roast
- salt and pepper, to taste

Wash thoroughly and chop collard greens, taking stems off.

Cook in a slow cooker or on the stove for 1 1/2 days. Cook one day and place in refrigerator.

Continue cooking the next day.

Use bacon grease or leftover drippings of a pork roast. Salt and pepper to taste.

Sometimes Aunt Betty would cook them on the back porch in the slow cooker or on a hot plate. Her family loved them. A real treat at Thanksgiving.

When I asked Aunt Betty to tell me how she cooked her collards, she remembered something her husband, Uncle Jerry, told her. Whenever she mentioned cooking rutabaga turnips, he'd say, "No thanks. I had enough of those growing up." He would help Mama chop the turnips. They were hard to cut up, so they had to use an axe. He said she cooked them a lot. Mama said she cooked what the Lord and her daddy provided. They did have, from time to time, okra and green beans. "Daddy would go to Feckory's and get green beans." Funny, though, about the turnips. Mama still loves turnips to this very day!

AUNT SALLIE'S COPPER PENNIES

- 2 cans sliced carrots, well drained
- 1 large onion, thinly sliced
- 1 green pepper, sliced

Into a saucepan place:

- 1 can tomato soup
- 1/4 c salad oil
- 1 c sugar
- 2/3 c vinegar
- 1 t pepper
- 1 t salt

Bring to a boil and pour hot mixture over carrots, onion, and pepper in bowl.

Let cool, then refrigerate. Serve cold.

***

Many times throughout the years,
Mama told me, "You can learn
something from everybody you
meet."

***

AUNT ETHEL'S CORN CASSEROLE

- 2 cans Mexicorn
- 2 c Minute rice, cooked
- 1 onion, sautéed in butter
- 1 can cream of mushroom soup
- 1 c sharp cheddar cheese

Combine all ingredients in a greased casserole dish.
Bake until bubbly at 350 degrees.

***

*When company came, Mama told
me, "We had to put on the big pot and
the little one." They planned to cook a
big meal.*

***

AUNT BETTY'S FISH

Mama said that her other sister-in-law, Fred's Betty, could really cook fish. Uncle Fred loved to fish, as did all her brothers. Aunt Betty could cook up "a mess of fish" like nobody else.

***

When I was ten, in church that Sunday morning, after the sermon and during the altar call, I looked up at Mama and asked, "Can I go?" Mama told me I could. Then she told me, after I prayed to receive Christ, now tell them you want to be baptized. I did, and one week later I was baptized. I remember that day like it was yesterday. Aunt Grace made me a new skirt to wear for the baptism.

Soon after, Mama told me that "Sweet Hour of Prayer" was her favorite hymn and she taught it to me.

***

GREEN BEANS

String the beans, break off each end, and break into small pieces.

Cover completely with water.

Cook with a small piece of salt pork, streak of lean, or butter.

Cook for 1 hour, stirring occasionally.

Add potatoes, peeled and cut up, and cook for 15 minutes longer.

AUNT GENIE'S NOODLES

When Aunt Genie made a beef roast, she always made noodles to go with it. They were simple to make, but still took practice to get them right. This makes a very stiff dough.

- 1 c plain flour
- 1/2 t salt
- 2 T cold water
- 1 egg, beaten

On a floured surface, roll out the dough, making it very thin.

Let stand 20 minutes.

Cut noodles into 1/4-inch by 2-inch pieces.

Drop the noodles into a pot with boiling beef broth. Cook for 10 minutes.

***

Mama told me,
"Time changes everything."

***

FRIED OKRA

- 1 lb okra
- 1 c cornmeal
- 1 T flour
- dash of salt
- 1/4 c Crisco or oil
- 1/4 stick butter

Wash and cut off ends of okra.

Slice and batter in cornmeal with a small amount of flour and a dash of salt.

Heat iron skillet. Add Crisco or oil, about 1/4 cup.

Brown okra and turn heat down and cover. Watch carefully and stir occasionally.

When brown, add 1/4 stick butter. Stir.

Place in oven at 375 for 15–20 minutes.

POTATO SALAD

- 6–8 medium potatoes
- 2 hardboiled eggs, chopped
- 1/4 t sugar
- 1 t yellow mustard
- 1/2 c chopped sweet pickles
- 1 c Miracle Whip salad dressing
- salt and pepper to taste

Wash, peel, and cut up potatoes.

Cover with water and cook for 20 minutes after they come to a boil.

Drain and let cool before mixing in other ingredients.

***

Just before I got married, Mama told me, "Just follow what the Bible says, and everything will be fine."

***

RUTABAGA TURNIPS

Mama said her daddy would bring home such large turnips that she couldn't handle it. She would get Jerry to chop it into fourths with an axe so then she could peel it and cut it into smaller pieces. Here's how Mama fixed hers.

- turnip
- salt pork
- salt

Peel and chop into 1/2-inch cubes.
Cover with water. Add a piece of salt pork.
Bring to a boil, then turn down on low and simmer for at least one hour.
Add salt to taste.

SALMON PATTIES

- 1 can of Double "Q" Pink Salmon (14.75 oz)
- 4 T cornmeal
- 3 T flour
- 1 egg
- 1 t baking soda
- 1/4 c buttermilk

Don't drain the salmon. Pick out skin and bones as you stir salmon.

Mix all ingredients thoroughly, pressing out the lumps.

Have skillet hot with bottom covered with oil.

Spoon salmon mixture into skillet.

Brown on both sides. Turn heat down and cook thoroughly.

SWEET POTATO SOUFFLÉ

- 2 c cooked, mashed sweet potatoes
- 1 c brown sugar
- 1/4 c sugar
- 1 stick butter
- 2 eggs

Mix all ingredients well and put in greased casserole dish. Cook at 325 for 30 minutes.

Topping:

- 2 cups cornflakes
- 3/4 stick butter
- 1 cup pecans, chopped

Roll cornflakes in a large bag to crush.
Melt butter and mix in cornflakes and pecans.
Spread on top of potatoes and cook 20 more minutes until light brown.
Freeze before topping and finish process later if not serving now.

***

*We have all heard Mama say many
times, "Come here and hug my neck."*

***

SQUASH CASSEROLE

- 2 lbs squash, sliced small
- 2 medium onions, chopped
- 16 oz sour cream
- 1 small can chopped water chestnuts
- 1/2 t salt
- 2 cans cream of chicken soup
- 1 c real butter
- 2 pkg Pepperidge Farm herb dressing mix

Cook squash and onions in a small amount of salted water until tender. Drain well.

Add soup, sour cream, and water chestnuts to squash.

Melt butter and add to dressing mix and stir.

Put 1/2 of dressing mix in bottom of baking dish. Add squash mixture, then put the rest of the dressing mix on top.

Bake at 350 for 30 minutes.

Serves 8 to 12.

Given to us by Suzanne Dobbs at the McDonald Reunion in July 1982.

TURKEY AND DRESSING

Mama always used an oven bag for her turkey. They always turned out moist and beautifully brown.

Follow the instructions that come with the bag. Using a bag makes it easy to drain the drippings by clipping a small hole in one corner of the bag.

Stew the giblets to make broth and use the broth and some of the drippings to put in the dressing.

Dressing:

- 1 pan of cornbread you made ahead
- 1 pkg Pepperidge Farm herb stuffing
- 5 biscuits or 5 slices of sandwich bread
- 2 hot dog buns
- 1 large onion
- 3 stalks of celery
- 2 t sage
- 2 t poultry seasoning
- salt and pepper, to taste
- 3 eggs

Mix all ingredients and add 3 cups of broth and 1 cup to 1 1/2 cups of the drippings. Mix thoroughly, adding more broth if needed. You want a consistency of cake batter.

Pour into baking pan and cook at 400 for 30–40 minutes.

Use the rest of the broth and some of the drippings to make gravy.

Put some flour in a glass and add water. Stir until lumps are gone and add to broth.

Add salt and pepper to taste and chopped boiled eggs.

Desserts

FRESH APPLE CAKE

- 1 c oil
- 1 t vanilla
- 3 eggs
- 5 apples, peeled and sliced
- 1 1/2 c sugar
- 1/2 c chopped nuts
- 1 t cinnamon
- 1/2 c raisins
- 2 c plain flour
- 1 t baking soda

Mix oil, eggs, and sugar together.
Add other ingredients.
Pour into greased 9x13 pan.
Bake for 45 minutes at 350.
Drizzle confectioner's sugar and water icing over top while cake is hot.

***

*When my boyfriend came over for
the first time, Mama told me, "Don't
let a boy know that you are anxious
to see him. Let him wonder."*

***

BANANA PUDDING

- 1/2 c sugar
- 2 T flour
- 1/4 t salt
- 2 c milk
- 3 egg yolks, save whites for meringue
- 1 t vanilla
- 6 medium ripe bananas, sliced
- vanilla wafers

Combine all except bananas and wafers. Stir until smooth over medium heat.

Line casserole dish with vanilla wafers and place in banana slices.

Pour filling over bananas and top with meringue.

Meringue:

- 1/4 cup sugar
- egg whites
- 1/4 teaspoon cream of tartar

Beat until stiff and cover filling.
Bake at 350 for about 12–15 minutes till golden brown.
Refrigerate.

AUNT BERNICE'S BLUEBERRY PIE

- 2 c blueberries
- 3/4 c sugar
- dash salt
- 1 T lemon juice
- 1 deep-dish pie shell, baked and cooled

Mix together 1/2 c water and 2 T cornstarch.
Add to blueberry mixture and heat until thick.
Let mixture cool before putting into pie shell.

***

One spring, Mama told her cousin,
"Look out there and see how green it's
gonna get." Her cousin just laughed
and asked Mama, "How can we see
how green it's gonna get?" Now every
spring we tell each other,
"Look how green it's gonna get."
An inside joke, I guess.

***

AUNT GRACE'S BLACK WALNUT EASY CAKE

- 1/2 c butter-flavored Crisco
- 1 1/3 c sugar
- 2 eggs
- 2 c self-rising flour
- 1 c milk
- 1 1/2 t vanilla

Cream Crisco and sugar together.
Add eggs, then add flour alternating with milk.
Add vanilla.
Pour into 2 greased and floured cake pans.
Bake at 300 for 30 minutes.

Icing:

- 3/4 c sugar
- 1 1/2 T cornstarch
- 1 c pineapple juice
- 2 T pineapple
- 1/4 stick butter
- 1 egg, beaten
- 1 c walnuts, chopped

Heat sugar, cornstarch, juice, pineapple, and butter until thick.
Add egg and cook long enough to cook egg.
Add walnuts, and spread on cake while cake is still hot.

Grace Stow made this for a Christmas party in 1989.

SELMA POWER'S CHOCOLATE PIE

- 2 c milk
- 1 c sugar
- 1/3 c flour
- 3 T cocoa
- 3 egg yolks, beaten, save whites for meringue
- pinch salt
- 1 t vanilla
- 2 T butter

Combine these ingredients in saucepan on medium heat, stirring until all lumps are gone.

Remove from stove.

When cooled, pour into a baked pie shell.

Meringue:

- egg whites
- 2 T sugar
- 1/4 t cream of tartar

Beat mixture until stiff. Don't beat too much.

Cover filling and bake at 350 for about 12–15 minutes till golden brown.

Refrigerate.

CREAM CHEESE CUPCAKES

- 3 8-oz pkgs cream cheese
- 5 eggs
- 1 c sugar
- 1 1/3 t vanilla

Cream the cream cheese at room temperature.
Add the eggs one at a time.
Add sugar and vanilla.
Fill cupcake papers 3/4 to 2/3 full.
Bake at 325 for 30 minutes, just as tops are browning. Watch carefully!
While they are baking, mix topping and set aside.

Topping:

- 1 c sour cream
- 1/2 c sugar
- strawberry jam

Spread a thin layer of topping over cupcakes, and in the center of each one, put a small amount of strawberry jam.
Place back in oven for 5 minutes, then chill.
Freezes well.

EGG CUSTARD

- 3 eggs
- 1 c sugar
- 2 T cornstarch
- 3/4 c PET evaporated milk
- 1 t vanilla
- 2 T butter

Bake crust for about 5 minutes before filling it.
Combine all ingredients and bake for 45 minutes at 350.
2 T of cocoa can be added to make a chocolate pie.

***

When talking about being frugal,
Mama told me, "Remember, you can
nickel-and-dime your money away."

***

FOUR-TIERED DELIGHT

- 1 1/2 c flour
- 1 1/2 sticks butter, melted
- 1 c chopped nuts

Mix these three ingredients and make a crust in the bottom of a sheet cake pan.

Cook at 350 for 15–20 minutes. Cool.

- 8 oz cream cheese
- 8 oz Cool Whip
- 1 c powdered sugar

Mix and pour on cooled crust.

- 2 pkgs of instant chocolate-pudding mix
- 3 c milk

Mix and pour over cream cheese mixture. Top with Cool Whip.

May add chocolate curls or nuts on top. Refrigerate.

***

*When things don't go your way,
Mama told me, "Bite your tongue. It
always works out, just let it take care
of itself."*

***

FRIED PIES

- 6 oz bag of dried apples (I found some in the produce section at Walmart)
- 3 T butter
- 3/4 c sugar
- cinnamon (optional)
- canned biscuits (or make dough as for biscuits)

Stew apples in water. Stir until apples *almost* reach applesauce consistency.

Add butter and sugar.

Roll out the dough the size of saucers.

Place the apple mixture in the center. Don't put too much.

Fold in half. Seal the edges by pressing down with a fork.

Then fry them in oil, browning on each side.

Drain on paper towel.

If you stew the apples the day before and refrigerate, they will handle better, and the time involved is shortened the day you fry them.

***

The first time she saw Joe McDonald
working at Reeves Food Town,
Mama told me, "If I were a young
girl, I'd set my hat for that boy!"
A couple of years later, I did.

***

LEMON PIE

- 1 box lemon pie filling

Follow directions on box, cooking until thick.

Graham Cracker Pie Crust:

- 9 graham crackers
- 1 stick of butter

Place graham crackers in pie pan.

Crumble the crackers, and then with a fork finish grinding the crackers until fine.

Melt 1 stick butter.

Pour melted butter in, and with fork spread and mold crackers to cover the sides and bottom of pie pan.

Pour cooled filling into pan.

Meringue:

- 3 egg whites
- 1/4 c sugar
- 1/4 t cream of tartar
- 1/2 t vanilla

Beat egg whites, cream of tartar, and vanilla until soft peaks, then gradually add in sugar until stiff peaks form.

Cover filling and bake at 350 for about 12–15 minutes till golden brown.

Refrigerate.

PECAN PIE

- 3 eggs
- 1 t vanilla
- 1/2 c sugar
- 1 c pecans
- 1 c dark Karo syrup
- 1/2 t salt

Mix these ingredients and pour into pie shell. Bake at 300 for 40–50 minutes.

***

My brother told me that Mama used to say, "Pull that door to." They got a kick out of that one at the University of Georgia.

***

AUNT LELIA POWER'S MAGIC POTATO COBBLER

- 2 1/2 c water
- 2 or 3 sweet potatoes, cut into strips

Cook over medium heat.

Batter:

- 1 c sifted flour
- 1/2 c sugar
- 2 t baking powder
- 1/4 t salt
- 1/2 c milk
- 1/4 c Crisco or butter (not margarine)

Mix dry ingredients together and cut the Crisco or butter into the flour mixture.

Pour into greased baking dish.

Lift out potato strips with fork and place on the batter, then mix the following ingredients and add to the water you cooked the potatoes in.

- 1 1/4 c sugar
- 2/3 stick of butter
- 1 c coconut
- 1 t orange or vanilla flavoring

Pour this mixture over potatoes.

Bake at 375 for 35 minutes or until golden brown.

Can substitute any fruit for potatoes. Coconut optional.

QUICKIE PIE

- 1 can of fruit (any kind)
- 1 c milk
- 1 stick butter
- 1 c sugar
- 1 c flour

Melt butter in pie pan.
Mix sugar and flour, then add fruit and milk.
Pour into pan and don't stir.
Bake at 375 for 45 minutes.

***

When Mama is about to give her
opinion on something, she says, "Well,
really and truly . . ."

***

AUNT BETTY'S POUND CAKE

- 3 c plain flour
- 5 eggs
- 1 c milk
- 2 3/4 c sugar
- 2 sticks butter
- 1 c Crisco
- 2 t vanilla

Mix all ingredients and place in a greased and floured tube cake pan.

Bake at 300 for 1 1/2 hours.

This is Uncle Charlie's wife's recipe.

CHOCOLATE POUND CAKE
(Originally called Fudge Pound Cake)

- 1 c Crisco
- 1/2 t baking powder
- 1 cup butter (2 sticks)
- 1/4 t salt
- 3 c sugar
- 1/2 c cocoa
- 5 eggs
- 1 c milk
- 3 c plain flour
- 1 T vanilla

Cream together Crisco, butter, and sugar. Then add eggs.

Sift together flour, salt, baking powder, and cocoa. Add this to cream mixture.

Add milk and vanilla.

Put in greased and floured tube cake pan.

Bake at 350 for 1 1/2 hours.

GERMAN CHOCOLATE CAKE

For my birthday, every year up until recently, Mama made a German chocolate cake from scratch. She used Baker's German Sweet Chocolate using the recipe on the inside of the wrapper. Delicious!

***

*Mama told me many times, "I reckon
all we can do is pray."*

***

QUINCE PIE

Just an added note:

Thinking back to Christmastime, Mama remembers her sister Bernice telling her how Grandma Power would walk a long distance from her place at Power's Ferry to Aunt Georgia Ann's place, at Crossroads and Dupree Street, near Crossroads School, to get enough quince to make a quince pie for Christmas. Since Aunt Bernice lived with Aunt Georgia Ann, Mama knew this to be true. Aunt Bernice said Grandma made one every Christmas. It was part of her traditions. A quince is a very hard fruit. It is so sour and could be used like any other fruit for a pie, but extra sugar might be needed.

***

My daughter, Donna, told me that
Mama told her, "Things will work
themselves out. Sometimes you have
just got to let the dominoes fall." She
said she uses it a lot.

***

About the Author

Joyce House McDonald has lived in the Atlanta, Georgia, area all her life, except for the eight years she and her husband lived in Baytown, Texas, and Humble, Texas. She is a founding member of Fellowship Bible Church in Roswell. She taught Precept Bible studies for seventeen years. She retired after twenty years with the Fulton County Board of Education as an elementary school paraprofessional. She is a widow with two children and six grandchildren. She and her mother currently reside in Cumming, Georgia. This is her first book.

1967: Joseph Lamar McDonald and Joyce House McDonald